NISTIR 7533

Manufacturing Interoperability Program, a Synopsis

Sharon J. Kemmerer
Manufacturing Systems Integration Division
Manufacturing Engineering Laboratory

February 2009

U.S. Department of Commerce
Gary Locke, Secretary

National Institute of Standards and Technology
Patrick D. Gallagher, Deputy Director

Table of Contents

FIGURES .... - 5 -

1. BACKGROUND .... - 6 -

2. INTRODUCTION .... - 6 -
   IMPORTANCE OF INTEROPERABILITY .... - 7 -
   NIST'S ROLE IN MANUFACTURING INTEROPERABILITY .... - 7 -
   MANUFACTURING INTEROPERABILITY PROGRAM DRIVERS .... - 7 -
       U.S. companies face major information barriers to global commerce .... - 7 -
       Industry Wants a Persistent Interoperability Testing Infrastructure .... - 9 -
       U.S. Government Has Identified Integrated Manufacturing Systems As Critical .... - 10 -
   TECHNICAL APPROACH .... - 11 -

3. INDUSTRY ENGAGEMENT .... - 14 -
   MANUFACTURING INTEROPERABILITY STRATEGY TEAM .... - 14 -
       Key Findings by MIST .... - 14 -
       MIST Workshop Recommendations .... - 15 -
   AUTOMOTIVE INDUSTRY ACTION GROUP .... - 16 -
       Inventory Visibility & Interoperability .... - 16 -
       ATHENA Project .... - 16 -
       B2B Testbed .... - 18 -
       MOSS Project .... - 20 -
       Metrology Interoperability Testbed .... - 23 -

4. ENGAGEMENT WITH OTHER GOVERNMENT AGENCIES .... - 24 -
   GENERAL SERVICES ADMINISTRATION .... - 24 -
   INTERNAL REVENUE SERVICE .... - 24 -
   ARMY .... - 25 -
       TARDEC .... - 25 -
       Army Future Combat Systems .... - 26 -
   NAVY CHIEF INFORMATION OFFICE .... - 26 -
   DOD SYSTEMS SOFTWARE & ENGINEERING OFFICE .... - 27 -
   UN/CEFACT .... - 29 -

5. RESULTS AND IMPACT .... - 29 -
   SEMANTIC RESEARCH CONTRIBUTIONS .... - 29 -
       AMIS .... - 29 -
       Reasoners .... - 30 -
   INFORMATION MODELS .... - 30 -
       Information Model for Machine Shop .... - 30 -
       Information Model for Product Representation .... - 31 -
   STANDARDS DEVELOPMENT AND ENHANCEMENTS .... - 32 -
       Systems Modeling Language (SysML) .... - 32 -
       Ontology Definition Metamodel (ODM) .... - 33 -
       Unified Modeling Language (UML) .... - 34 -
       Meta-Object Facility (MOF) .... - 34 -
       Business Process Modeling Notation (BPMN) .... - 34 -
       Business Motivation Model (BMM) .... - 35 -
       Semantics of Business Vocabulary and Business Rules (SBVR) .... - 35 -
       Business Process Definition Metamodel (BPDM) .... - 35 -
       Process Specification Language (PSL) .... - 35 -
       OWL Web Ontology Language (OWL) .... - 36 -
       Semantic Web Services Language (SWSL) .... - 36 -
       Quality Measurement Data (QMD) .... - 37 -
       Dimensional Measurement Interface Standard (DMIS) .... - 37 -

Inspection Plus-Plus (I++) Dimensional Measurement Equipment (DME) Standard .... - 38 -
Core Manufacturing Simulation Data (CMSD) Specification .... - 39 -
Standard for the Exchange of Product model data (STEP) Standards .... - 40 -
TESTING & EVALUATION SUPPORT .... - 41 -
SEMANTIC TECHNOLOGY SUPPORT SOFTWARE .... - 44 -
Minimal Interface to Vampire (MIV) .... - 44 -
PSL's "20 Questions" .... - 44 -
Sumo2loom .... - 44 -
APPLICATION SUPPORT SOFTWARE .... - 45 -
Automating Equipment Information Exchange (AEX) Schemas .... - 45 -
Express Injector .... - 45 -
Expresso for Linux and Windows .... - 45 -
MANUFACTURING SIMULATION MODELS .... - 46 -
SPREADING THE WORD .... - 47 -
MIP-Related Workshop Highlights .... - 47 -

6. THE SPAWNING OF OTHER PROGRAMS .... - 50 -

SUSTAINABLE AND LIFECYCLE INFORMATION-BASED MANUFACTURING (SLIM) PROGRAM .... - 51 -
SUPPLY CHAIN INTEGRATION PROGRAM .... - 52 -

7. CONCLUSION .... - 53 -

8. ACKNOWLEDGEMENTS .... - 54 -

9. DISCLAIMER .... - 54 -

PUBLICATIONS .... - 55 -

Figures

Figure 1: 21st Century Manufacturing Environment .... - 8 -

Figure 2: MIP Customer Needs .... - 9 -

Figure 3: Manufacturing Interoperability Program Thrusts .... - 12 -

Figure 4: ATHENA Pilot Project High-Level Architecture .... - 18 -

Figure 5: B2B Testbed Methodology .... - 19 -

Figure 6: ATHENA Demonstration Pilot Using B2B Testbed .... - 20 -

Figure 7: MOSS Potential Failure Points in the Supply Chain .... - 21 -

Figure 8: MOSS Proof of Concept Scope .... - 22 -

Figure 9: MOSS Testbed .... - 22 -

Figure 10: Dimensional Metrology Standards Landscape .... - 23 -

Figure 11: IRS XML Framework for Design .... - 25 -

Figure 12: Examples of Plug Fest Exercises .... - 28 -

Figure 13: Validator Used in Plug Fest .... - 29 -

Figure 14: Concept for the Machine Shop Information Model .... - 31 -

Figure 15: SysML .... - 32 -

Figure 16: SysML and STEP .... - 33 -

Figure 17: The Impact of DMIS .... - 38 -

Figure 18: Dimensional Metrology Standards Landscape .... - 39 -

Figure 19: QOD Testing Environment .... - 43 -

Figure 20: QOD Authoring and Sharing Environment .... - 43 -

Figure 21: Screen Shot of the Minimal Interface to Vampire .... - 44 -

Figure 22: Expresso Example .... - 45 -

1. Background

With a value-added contribution of $1.5 trillion, U.S. manufacturing directly accounts for 14 percent of the U.S. gross domestic product.[1] Manufacturing plays a central role in our Nation's economy. Dollar for dollar, manufacturing has the highest economic impact of all of the economic sectors. Dollar for dollar, manufacturing has the highest-leverage economic impact of all of the economic sectors.[2] As such, manufacturing's ability to innovate and compete is vital to all the other sectors of the economy. Other facts attributable to manufacturing:

- makes the highest contribution to economic growth of any sector

- is responsible for more than 70 percent of private sector research and development and the center for a wide range of advanced technologies that cut energy use and lead to a cleaner environment

- achieves a high productivity rate year in and year out, increasing by more than 50 percent in the past decade

- contributes more than 60 percent of U.S. exports or about $50 billion a month

- pays wages and benefits that are about 25 percent higher than in non-manufacturing jobs

- multiplies every dollar spent into an additional $1.37 in economic activity, greater than other sectors.[3]

The National Institute of Standards and Technology (NIST) Manufacturing Engineering Laboratory (MEL) contributes to the innovation and competitiveness of U.S. manufacturing through measurement science, measurement services, and technical contributions to critical standards. MEL brings to bear considerable resources in support of U.S. manufacturing, including numerous unique facilities, and dedicated staff and associates. MEL serves the manufacturing sector of the U.S. economy in a broad sense, working with partners from industry as well as other government agencies and academia to develop the measurement tools and infrastructure that enable new products, higher productivity, and improved processes. When only a few months' lag in product development can jeopardize the financial health and stability of even the most established companies, manufacturers must have the resources to meet the demands of increased global competition and continue to make quality products meeting the needs of their customers. MEL actively anticipates these changing circumstances and pushes beyond the state of the art to the next generation of measurement and standard needs. In 2004 the MEL Management Council focused its work strategically to better ensure the future vitality, quality, and productivity of the laboratory's portfolio of technical programs. The Council assessed the technical direction and goals, the structure, and the operation of the entire MEL technical program portfolio, making changes as warranted by that assessment. The result was a refreshed portfolio that addressed the needs of our customers, aligned with NIST's strategic directions, and made maximum use of our technical capability. The Manufacturing Interoperability Program (MIP) was launched from this refreshed portfolio of programs.

2. Introduction

Started in 2005 through its wrap-up in 2008, the Manufacturing Interoperability Program has seen an annual investment of roughly 25-30 fulltime staff who have researched, developed, and deployed standards, tools, techniques, and testing environments --- helping manufacturing enterprise systems to integrate more easily. Program management, leadership, and strategic direction was set by the Manufacturing Systems Integration Division's (MSID) Chief. With a budget of $4-6 million annually, the goal of MIP was to equip U.S.

---

1 "Subcommittee on U.S. Competitiveness Focus: R&D --- Innovation, Technology, Process, and Advancement of Knowledge," The Manufacturing Council, Washington DC 20230, November 5, 2005.
2 *U.S. Department of Commerce Bureau of Economic Analysis, Industry-by-Industry Total Requirements after Redefinitions (1997 to 2006).* Available at: http://www.bea.gov/industry/iotables/table_list.cfm?anon=66870
3 "The Facts about Modern Manufacturing, 7th Edition," The Manufacturing Institute, October 2006.

manufacturers with the technical guidance and testing support needed to interoperate in today's global, heterogeneous manufacturing world.

Importance of Interoperability

MIP focused on "interoperability" across manufacturing systems and processes for effective communication of data and information. You'll learn more about the role staff played in working the issues to progress effective communication in both syntactic and semantic interoperability.[4]

Interoperability is essential to the productivity and competitiveness of many industries. Premised on a reliable digital representation of product and process data coordinated by many different participants and processes, interoperability is necessary for efficient design, production, and supply chain management. NIST has produced several studies quantifying the costs of inadequate and inefficient interoperability in the automotive, electronics, and construction industries. These studies can be found at:
http://www.mel.nist.gov/msidlibrary/impact_studies.html .
Effective interoperability is impacted by several factors, which include:

- Attempting data exchange between commercially similar or dissimilar systems.
- Attempting data exchange between same-vendor software but with different versions on each machine.
- Upward and downward compatibility between software versions.
- Misinterpreting definitions or the meaning of terms used to structure data exchange or interpret the meaning of that which is exchanged.
- Not using a recognized normative documentary standard upon which exchange data is formatted and based.
- No means of consistently testing self-declared conformant applications to ensure correct communication, one system to the other.

NIST's Role in Manufacturing Interoperability

Why NIST? NIST is a neutral, non-regulatory agency. It provides an open, rigorous process for developing metrics, standards, and testing methods without preconceived notions. MIP provided the infrastructure for NIST staff to collaborate with industry to develop and test open standards and specifications that support manufacturing industry requirements for interoperability. Researchers worked with national and international standards development bodies and foreign government agencies to normalize accreditation and certification requirements, facilitated standards convergence, and participated in pilot programs to prove out new specifications and business processes. MIP established a testing and demonstration environment with an adaptable infrastructure. You'll read more about our partnerships and work later in this document.

Manufacturing Interoperability Program Drivers

U.S. COMPANIES FACE MAJOR INFORMATION BARRIERS TO GLOBAL COMMERCE

Globalization is the major trend in manufacturing today—globalization of markets and globalization of partners. "Accelerated competition at home and the growing sophistication of developing markets will have driven manufacturers increasingly to source, manufacture and sell internationally. By 2020, around 80% of manufacturers expect to have multi-country operations whereas currently just over half do."[5] The globalization of markets means that companies want to build and sell their products from all over the world. The globalization of partners means

---

[4] Syntactic interoperability involves a common data format and common protocol to structure anything that is ambiguous, and communicate for purposes of resolving ambiguities in the structure. Semantic Interoperability is the ability of two or more computer systems to exchange information and have the meaning of that information automatically interpreted by the receiving system accurately enough to produce useful results, as defined by the end users of both systems. http://en.wikipedia.org/wiki/Semantic_interoperability

[5] "Manufacturing in 2020, Envisioning a Future Characterised by Increased Internationalisation, Collaboration and Complexity," Capgemini & IDG Global Solutions, December 2008.

that supply chain members that support a manufacturing enterprise are also located worldwide. Both have led to an explosion in the amount of information sharing that must take place, magnifying the necessity for accurate and timely visibility of the supply chain. Acknowledged poor information visibility in the supply chain results in unnecessary inventory. In the 2006 State of Logistics Report for the Council of Supply Chain Management Professionals, economist Rosalyn A. Wilson writes that logistics costs have increased 15.2 percent from 2004 to 2005. A big component of that increase is the cost of carrying inventory, which has increased by $61 billion in the United States. In NIST's 2004 study, Economic Impact of Inadequate Infrastructure for Supply Chain Integration estimated the total annual costs of inadequacies in supply chain infrastructures to be in excess of $5 billion/year for the automotive industry, and almost $3.9 billion/year for the electronics industry.[6]

The inability to integrate business information seamlessly and automatically is at the heart of all of these issues. A $1 reduction in cost from supply chain efficiencies is equivalent to a $12 increase in sales revenues.[7] The production of complex products like cars, planes, and buildings requires integration across several supply chains. It is absolutely critical to the success of companies and their suppliers that this sharing is done correctly, efficiently, and inexpensively. Figure 1, from the Integrated Manufacturing Technology Initiative's roadmap, "Technologies for Enterprise Integration,"[8] characterizes the many influences on the manufacturing environment in the 21st century.

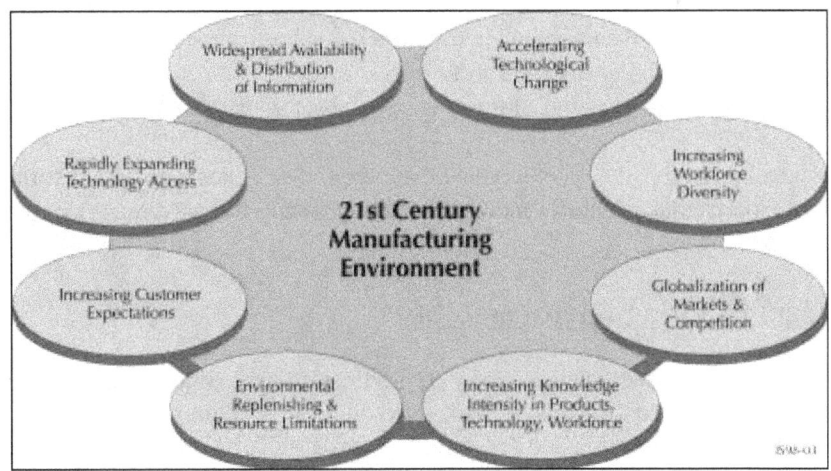

Figure 1: 21st Century Manufacturing Environment

Changes in technology, from faster networks to new computer languages such as eXtensible Markup Language (XML)9, are impacting the way in which this information sharing takes place.

The Semantic Web's10 advent has also been a prevailing influence on today's information dissemination and communication. Simply stated, the Semantic Web will enable computers to understand the meaning of concepts, to reason about those concepts, and act on those concepts according to the rules they have been given. This requires a new type of programming language that deals directly and only with the semantics of the information. The resulting computer programs will operate at the semantic level, not the data level. As it relates to manufacturing, these programs will know that purchase orders are different from schedules, which in turn are different from numerical control (NC) programs; and they will know how to deal with those differences.

The Internet and electronic commerce changed the way many businesses operate, but this may be just the tip of the

---

6 Economic Impact of Inadequate Infrastructure for Supply Chain Integration, Planning Report 04-2, June 2004. http://www.nist.gov/director/prog-ofc/report04-2.pdf
7 Ryder Center for Supply Chain Management, Florida International University: http://business.fiu.edu/centers/ryder.cfm
8 http://web.archive.org/web/20040408100723/www.imti21.org/enterprise_integration.htm
9 http://www.w3.org/XML/
10 http://infomesh.net/2001/swintro/

iceberg. The Semantic Web has the potential to produce enormous benefits to manufacturing as well as generate new challenges. Many questions must be addressed. What types of interface standards, modeling tools, and test methods will be needed tomorrow to capture and exchange the semantics that these new computer programs will use to do these wonderful things? What types of standards, tools, and methods are needed by customers to deal with today's technology? Which of the emerging standards provide the needed functionality for new advanced applications? Just how well do new software systems conform to these new standards?

Solving this cross-cutting integration problem requires a common standards and measurement infrastructure, which NIST is uniquely positioned to address for these many issues facing industry. As you will read in the following pages, MIP helped industry and government to reduce barriers for interoperability. As an example, our testing service to this customer base is best illustrated in Figure 2.

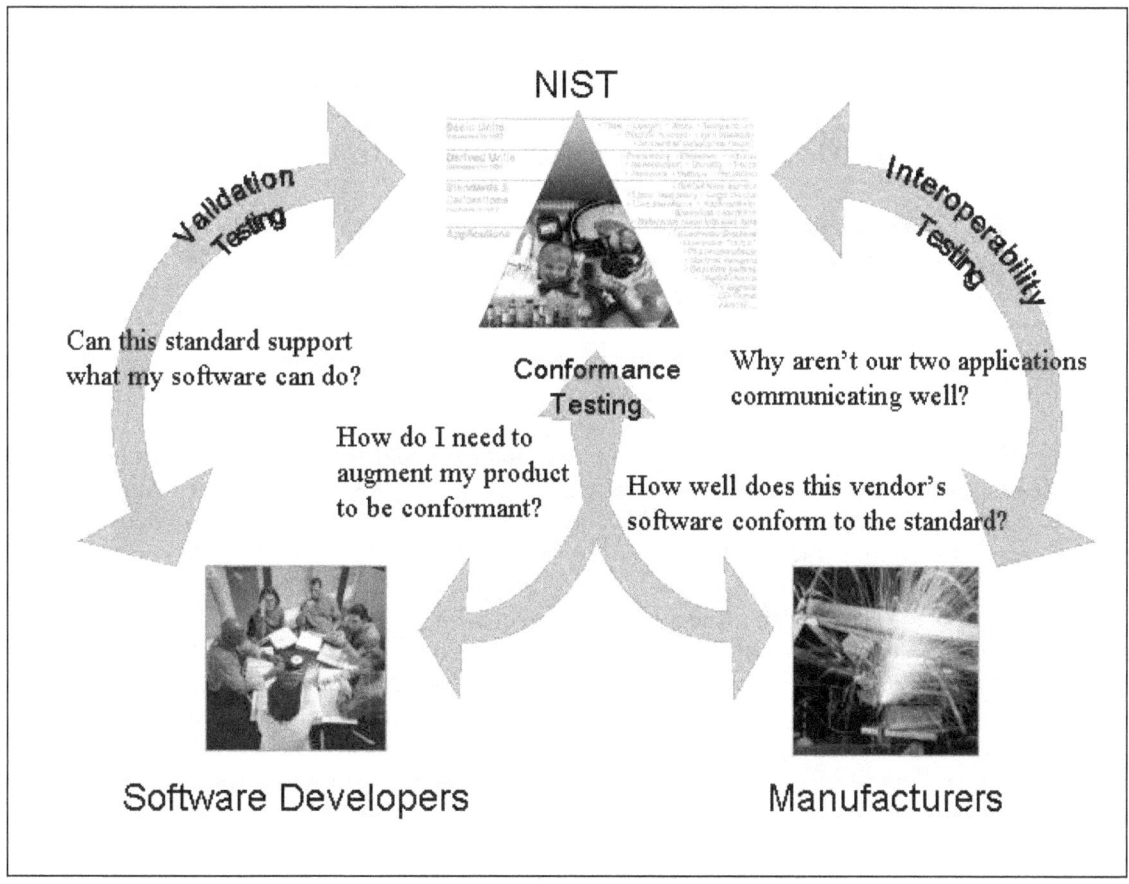

Figure 2: MIP Customer Needs

INDUSTRY WANTS A PERSISTENT INTEROPERABILITY TESTING INFRASTRUCTURE

To get to system interoperability across the infrastructure requires focused testing at several different levels:

- Validation testing - for standards development
- Conformance testing – for evaluating implementations of standards against the standard's requirements
- Interoperability testing – assessing the ability of conforming implementations to exchange information with each other

From the following testimonials, one can see that NIST is positioned to help industry:

"NIST is doing what our industry members won't do – providing the infrastructure and testing resources to speed the development and implementation of new specifications." David Connelly, President, Open Applications Group

"No one company can expect to enforce a coherent set of de facto standards that all other companies will fall into line with." "...our role is quite distinct from that of NIST, who we believe can and should aspire to represent the neutral viewpoint and broker for real-world interoperability testing and conformance supporting the needs of specific industries such as Automotive [sic] who are trying to make interoperable communications between business partners real." Charles Johnson, Managing Director, Manufacturing Industry, Microsoft Corporation

NIST's involvement in testing AIAG's proposed standards "is absolutely essential to delivering quality projects to automotive supply chain." Pat Snack, Director of Technical Programs, Automotive Industry Action Group (AIAG)

U.S. GOVERNMENT HAS IDENTIFIED INTEGRATED MANUFACTURING SYSTEMS AS CRITICAL

In 1999 NIST estimated that inadequate interoperability of engineering data alone, cost the automotive supply chain $1 billion per year. ... Why does a problem identified as significant more than five years ago continue to bedevil the manufacturing verticals? How are software suppliers addressing this challenge? What are manufacturers doing to cope?

Driven by such predictions as a 2001 forecast on relevant market growth:

"The Enterprise Integration market will reach over $11 billion by 2006, growing at a Compound Annual Growth Rate (CAGR) of 20%. Market growth in manufacturing industries has been driven by the need to accommodate new business models where supply chain management techniques, partner relationships, customer service, and others make external integration a requirement."[11]

The government's awareness of the cost burden associated with inadequate interoperability shifted to action when Congress passed the Enterprise Integration Act of 2002. The Act was agreed to by both House and Senate and signed into Public Law 107–277 on November 5, 2002. The Act was established *"To authorize the National Institute of Standards and Technology to work with major manufacturing industries on an initiative of standards development and implementation for electronic enterprise integration."* Interoperability across systems and platforms would result if enterprises were integrated. Key to the need for enterprise integration are the findings spelled out by the Public Law:

(1) Over 90 percent of United States companies engaged in manufacturing are small- and medium-sized businesses.
(2) Most of these manufacturers produce goods for assemblage into products of large companies.
(3) The emergence of the World Wide Web and the promulgation of international standards for product data exchange greatly accelerated the movement toward electronically integrated supply chains during the last half of the 1990's.
(4) European and Asian countries are investing heavily in electronic enterprise standards development, and in preparing their smaller manufacturers to do business in the new environment. European efforts are well advanced in the aerospace, automotive, and shipbuilding industries and are beginning in other industries including home building, furniture manufacturing, textiles, and apparel. This investment could give overseas companies a major competitive advantage.
(5) The National Institute of Standards and Technology, because of the electronic commerce expertise in its laboratories and quality program, its long history of working cooperatively with manufacturers, and the

---

11 Bob Mick, Vice President ARC Advisory Group, "Enterprise Integration Market to Reach $11 Billion," ARC Advisory Group - ARCweb - 23 October 2001.

nationwide reach of its manufacturing extension program, is in a unique position to help United States large and smaller manufacturers alike in their responses to this challenge.

(6) It is, therefore, in the national interest for the National Institute of Standards and Technology to accelerate its efforts in helping industry develop standards and enterprise integration processes that are necessary to increase efficiency and lower costs.

Although no new funds were appropriated in support of Public Law 107-277, government agencies continued to prevail with the message that solutions to improve interoperability are crucial if we are to remain competitive and dissolve inefficiencies within our enterprises. The following are a short list of examples from this crusade:

- *"Interoperability is a cornerstone of [the Navy Department's] efforts to strengthen its independent operations and, subsequently, improve the warfighter's ability to find, retrieve, process and exchange information,"* Wennergren said in a December 13, 2002 statement to Navy commanders. *"The department, like many government and private-sector organizations, has increasingly looked to XML technology to meet its data sharing needs." The policy's overall goals are to promote XML as a technology to help achieve interoperability throughout the Navy and serve as a guideline to support interoperability among the Navy and other DOD components."*[12]

- In March 2003, during National Manufacturing Week, [then] Department of Commerce Secretary Evans announced the President's Manufacturing Initiative in a speech before the National Association of Manufacturers in Chicago. Secretary Evans ordered a comprehensive review of the issues influencing long-term competitiveness of U.S. manufacturing. The Manufacturing Initiative is a series of 57 recommendations taken from discussions with U.S. manufacturers during 23 public roundtables held by the Commerce Department between April and September 2003. The result is an 88-page report, Manufacturing in America, released on January 16, 2004.

- The 2004 Commerce Department report, Manufacturing in America, recommended the creation of the Interagency Working Group (IWG) on Manufacturing Research and Development (R&D) to identify and integrate R&D requirements and to develop strategies for the Federal Government's manufacturing R&D programs. The IWG on Manufacturing R&D reported to the National Science and Technology Council (NSTC), Committee on Technology, and was chaired by the Director of the MEL at the NIST. Its membership included representatives from 15 federal agencies. Key issues for manufacturing were identified,[13] and a few aligned closely with the intent of the Manufacturing Interoperability Program:
  - *"In an increasingly globalized economy, the capacity to compete successfully will depend on the ability of individual manufacturers to satisfy global as well as U.S. standards."*[14]
  - *"There are no easy answers to these questions -nor is there an easy answer to any one interoperability problem. This problem is so widespread that many products are not even backward compatible with themselves, let alone other systems."* [15]

Past President George W. Bush believed in the need for integration and advancement in the manufacturing supply chain to improve productivity. His American Competitiveness Initiative Act (ACI) stated: "While expected new innovations are impossible to predict with specificity, certain capabilities and technology platforms can be anticipated as a result of ACI: [NIST's] Development of manufacturing standards for the supply chain to advance and accelerate the development and integration of more efficient production practices."[16]

Technical Approach

MSID's aim is to equip today's manufacturer with the guidance and testing support needed to participate in the global, distributed manufacturing world. Through MIP, we worked with industrial partners to overcome

---

12 FCWCOM - Federeal Computer Week - 18 December 2002
13 www.manufacturing.gov
14 http://www.manufacturing.gov/keyissues/standards.asp?dName=keyissues
15 Government Computer News - GCN.com - Alice Lipowicz - 10/03/2005
16 Bush, George W., "American Competitiveness Initiative," January 31, 2006, http://www.whitehouse.gov/stateoftheunion/2006/aci/ .

information-handling barriers. These barriers have arisen from the increased reliance on electronic information exchange across systems, and with distant customers and suppliers. Using a virtual manufacturing environment where vendors and manufacturers can test conformance to existing standards, and researchers can validate the next generation of standards is one of the many contributions MIP provided the manufacturing industry.

Program Thrusts - The Manufacturing Interoperability Program focused on three major thrusts:

A. An interoperability testing and demonstration infrastructure
B. Testing of key integration standards for today's manufacturers
C. Development of semantic technologies for tomorrow's integration needs

As shown in Figure 3, these three thrusts depend on one another to be successful. Integration standards were identified in concert with industrial partners for key manufacturing areas such as product, process, operations, and supply chains.

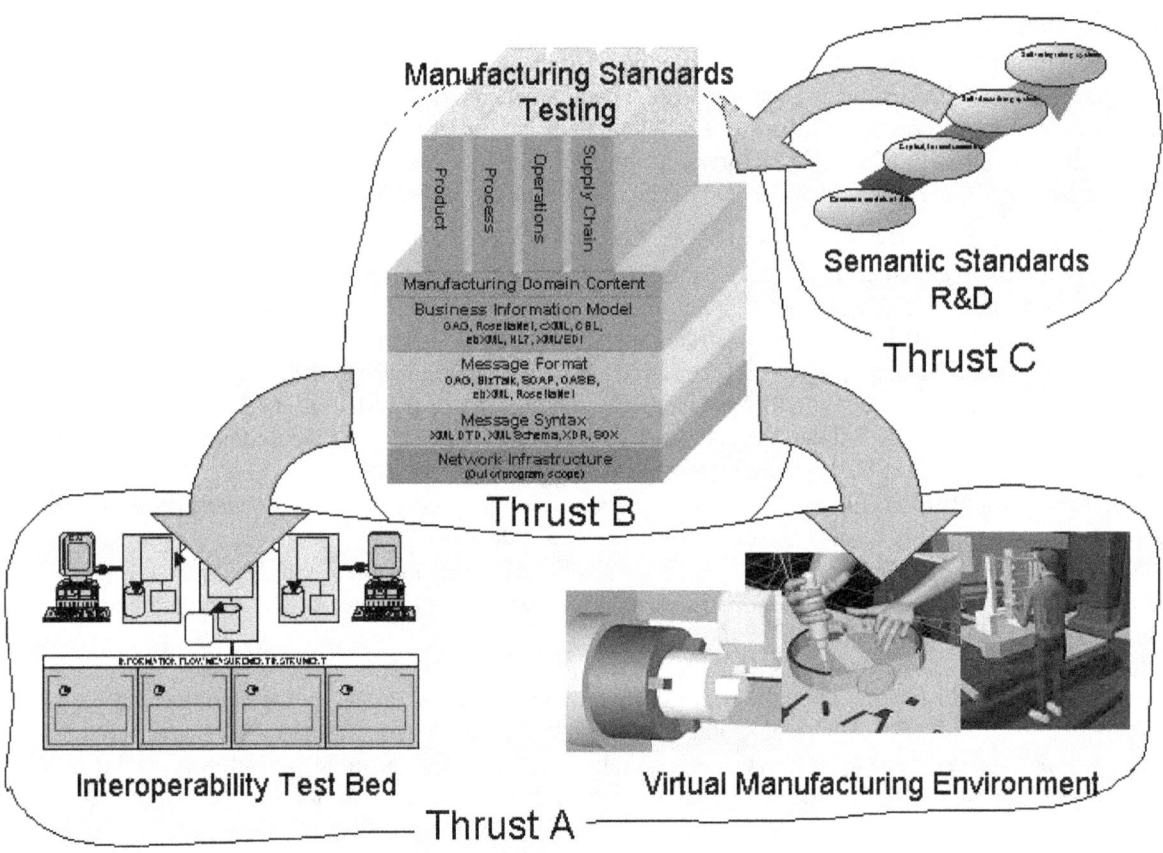

Figure 3: Manufacturing Interoperability Program Thrusts

Thrust A - Interoperability Testing and Demonstration Infrastructure

This infrastructure built upon past efforts and collaborations initiated under earlier MEL programs and projects that addressed interoperability testing and the simulation of manufacturing supply chains, systems, and processes. MIP enhanced an existing Business-to-Business (B2B) Testbed that provided a consistent testing framework and tools for standards conformance and interoperability demonstration. Associated tools developed as part of this project and the B2B Testbed itself are highlighted later in this report. Identified standards were applied within the interoperability testing and demonstration infrastructure, which contained two major components:

- A testing environment for logging, diagnosis, conformance, and interoperability testing focused at the content level.
- A piloting and demonstration environment populated with commercial production software tools to establish the usability of these standards-based approaches in realistic settings.

Thrust B – Integration Standards Testing

A typical interaction between a manufacturer and a customer or supplier contains a minimal set of technical information, often called a technical data package. This information includes a specification of a product to be manufactured along with quality specifications and at times processing requirements. The manufacturer in turn must incorporate this manufacturing need into its ongoing operation plans – schedules, inventory, resource, and component requirements. By focusing on just this minimal set of requirements, we identified cross-referencing standards needed to support a majority of manufacturers, especially small manufacturers. These standards, illustrated in Figure 3, must be compatible with one another to enable smooth information flow across the manufacturing domains of product, process, operations and the supply chain. This program identified and validated such standards by teaming with industrial partners in a collaborative environment.

The specifications, typical software applications, and associated test data were validated using testing tools such as those within the B2B Testbed. Several real world test case data sets were established in cooperation with industrial and research collaborators. Testbed tools were built to support information modeling, file wrapper development and deployment, system prototyping, verification; and validation, conformance, and interoperability testing.

Thrust C – Development of New Technologies for Interoperability Standards and Integration

MIP also invested in a strong research thrust to support the use of semantic technologies in new standards. It is becoming widely accepted that semantic technology is the correct way to transmit information in an unambiguous and computable fashion. There are two overarching drivers for semantics technology:

- Need for more rigor (less ambiguity) in exchange standards.
- Rapid growth in the number of standards needed. Thus we must automate systems integration as much as possible.

This thrust addressed the fundamental research necessary for information system development to move to a new level of information exchange, and for MIP to facilitate automation and the integration of industry's next generation of systems.

Semantic approaches are the next logical step in bringing computer languages closer to the way business, engineering, and manufacturing experts understand their problems. These approaches express the expert's concepts in terms of meaningful, computable statements. The techniques are not oriented toward computational speed, but rather precision of expression. In this way, the specific conclusions or effects that are expected of the system can be recorded, validated with automated reasoning and simulation, and used to verify the performance of the system built. Its semantic description can be searched by others looking for existing functionality to reuse, or can be automatically composed with semantic descriptions of other systems to create newly integrated ones. The semantic description can also be used to present the data in the system in a way domain experts can understand, and enable automated and semi-automated decision-making. MSID has several staff who are recognized leaders in this arena.

3. Industry Engagement

Manufacturing Interoperability Strategy Team

On May 19, 2005, the MIP Manager hosted a Manufacturing Interoperability Strategy Team (MIST) Workshop at NIST. Team participants represented senior executives from industry, technology consortia, and government agencies. The objective of the workshop was to elicit input from participants about needs, challenges, and priorities each are confronting in the context of manufacturing interoperability. Participants discussed barriers to interoperability, critical needs for their industry sector, and future technology trends affecting or relating to interoperable systems. Participants were asked to review MIP and make specific recommendations regarding program objectives, priorities, and technical activities.

For the workshop, interoperability was defined as, "The ability of applications and systems to share information and exchange services with each other based on standards, and to cooperate in processes using the information and services." Successful interoperability is when different applications, working independently, can exchange information and this information is understood by each system involved in the exchange. Workshop participants discussed problems and barriers to interoperability and implementation of integration solutions. None of the participants believed that the necessary framework is in place today to achieve the desired level of interoperability across the entire enterprise, and more research and development are needed.

KEY FINDINGS BY MIST

The MIST workshop participants identified several areas of consensus across domains and focus areas:

Diverse Sectors Share Common Integration Needs

Workshop participants noted that many sectors beyond manufacturing share common information technology needs, interoperability challenges, and integration requirements. These include not only similar industry sectors, such as construction, electronics, and chemical processing; but also service sectors, such as, government, healthcare, legal, and financial.

Overlapping Standards Inhibit Adoption

Participants agreed that there is a significant level of frustration with overlapping standards. U.S. companies are global companies with a global supply chain that mandates interaction across systems and industries that apply standards from all over the world. Companies will not buy standard solutions without a market, and software providers need the industry groups to make the market for the standard before they will implement it. Participants agreed that an attempt needs to be made to bring many of these efforts together. An example is the European Union's ATHENA[17] project, introduced later in this report.

Business Case Development Is Insufficient

Several workshop participants stressed the need for business case development resources. Participants acknowledged the NIST interoperability cost studies as excellent references for building business cases. However, participants agreed that a common set of metrics is also needed to assess the value of manufacturing (or any other) interoperability investments. Expenditures for interoperability improvements must be justifiable in a business context, such as, "timeliness to mission" or "time to market." Lack of business metrics is a significant barrier to investment in interoperability technology and standards development.

Cross-Cutting Enablers have Potential for Greater Impact

Basic infrastructural technologies such as modeling and metadata applicable in many domain areas, have potential for wide impact. NIST's work on ontologies, Object Management Group (OMG) metadata standards, and Unified

---

[17] Advanced Technologies for Interoperability of Heterogeneous Enterprise Networks (ATHENA)

Modeling Language (UML) were cited as examples of cross-cutting enablers that contribute positive impact for manufacturers. Participants identified enterprise ontology development as a high priority. One participant stated that taxonomies are not enough; ontologies are needed to show relationships and lower order effects. Participants expressed the need for government funded research in this area to make advances in tool development and semantic validation techniques and to further integrate across the manufacturing enterprise.

Testbeds are Needed to Facilitate Implementation

A testbed includes specifications, software, hardware, package of instrumentation, business scenarios, test artifacts, and guidelines needed to facilitate technology evaluation experiments. Testbeds are designed to evaluate alternative or new application integration technologies, and to accelerate their maturation and transition into project use. Participants considered testbeds to be an indispensable component of the implementation and demonstration process for successful data exchange and system integration. However, several industry representatives stated the funding for establishing testbeds was very difficult to obtain because of the shared nature of the resource, and all that is required to build and maintain them. A neutral party provider of a testbed allows multiple industry partners to reduce their individual expense, to leverage the resources, and benefit from the demonstrated results.

MIST WORKSHOP RECOMMENDATIONS

Workshop participants concluded the workshop by developing a list of recommendations for the Manufacturing Interoperability Program based on findings and discussions at the workshop. Participants emphasized activities with the broadest possible impact. The following recommendations were not prioritized by the participants.

The Manufacturing Interoperability Program should:

- Focus on cross-cutting enablers rather than current application-specific areas, e.g., process, product, design, and supply chain. These enablers could be viewed as "functional threads across the MIP verticals." Interoperability requirements and methodologies are very similar among these application areas. If the NIST purpose is to enable, it should do that in a generic way to enable application across the manufacturing domains.

- Provide a holistic, high-level view on integrating various interoperability efforts (e.g., design, supply chain, production). MIP projects should move up a level to understand the relationship between standards. An analogy to this is the Open Systems Interconnection[18] stack that sorted out the relationships of network standards to each other, which helped lead to the Internet technology. A high level view would give some perspective to see how standards should fit together, and provide a gap analysis on what still needs to be done.

- Participate in international standards development and validation efforts such as ATHENA, an integrated project sponsored by the European Commission.[19]

- Help connect funded integration and interoperability research projects at NIST to projects occurring within industry.

- Develop a registry for interoperability standards, models, and tools that support both government and industry.

- Provide a framework for testing interoperable data exchange that can be publicly advertised to service providers and test participants; and maintain a persistent Testbed for interoperability. (Other countries are funding these activities at the government level and the United States should consider doing so as well.)

---

18 http://en.wikipedia.org/wiki/OSI_model
19 http://www.athena-ip.org/index.php?option=content&task=view&id=44&Itemid=89

Test methods and cases need to be documented and made publicly available to better ensure repeatability and measurable outcomes.

- Develop a strategic plan to effectively support interoperability testing for business systems integration.

- Continue in the semantic integration work. More research is needed in this area.

- (While not within MIP control), NIST should support consortia activities such as the Next Generation Manufacturing Technology Initiative20 and National Council for Advanced Manufacturing21 and provide input to the Interagency Working Group on Manufacturing. Common concerns across domains should be a focus for NIST involvement.

Automotive Industry Action Group

The Automotive Industry Action Group (AIAG) is a globally recognized organization founded in 1982 by a group of visionary managers from Chrysler, Ford, and General Motors. The purpose is to provide an open forum where members cooperate in developing and promoting solutions that enhance the prosperity of the automotive industry. AIAG's focuses on continuously improving business processes and practices involving trading partners throughout the supply chain.

Under the auspices of AIAG, volunteer members from all layers of the supply chain work together to resolve issues critical to the automotive supply chain.[22] While MEL and MSID have been collaboratively engaged in many standards development and supply chain improvement efforts with the AIAG over the years, the following activities within MIP directly influenced the collaborative relationship with the AIAG toward common interoperability solutions.

INVENTORY VISIBILITY & INTEROPERABILITY

AIAG has developed a standards-based approach to support cross-enterprise Inventory Visibility & Interoperability (IV&I) business processes by enabling interoperable IV&I applications. The NIST Manufacturing B2B Testbed was used to test a proof of concept and eventually an industry pilot. The project objectives were to:
- Define a model for general interoperability (business process and data models)
- Model the business process and create collaborations
- Define the architecture and framework to support messages created from a data model
- Run a proof of concept to test solutions

ATHENA PROJECT

New solutions to automate automotive business processes are built to connect disparate systems and require advanced data management technologies for effective interoperable systems development. AIAG and its member companies sought to validate a new generation of research tools from the European Union (EU)-funded research project ATHENA[23] on the task of inventory visibility tool integration. A technically capable organization was needed to authoritatively develop and direct the validation pilot. MIP staff provided, and managed execution of, a technical plan to validate the EU-funded ATHENA project tools based on the AIAG Inventory Visibility and Interoperability (IV&I) project requirements. The validation team was distributed geographically and consisted of

---

20 http://www.ngmti.org/
21 http://www.nacfam.org/
22 http://www.aiag.org/staticcontent/about/index.cfm?section=aiag
23 ATHENA, Advanced Technologies for Interoperability of Heterogeneous Enterprise Networks, is an EU Sixth framework project, which commenced on the 1st of January 2004, and which will propose the proper actions to be taken concerning the Digital Switchover (DSO) in UHF, (the transition form analogue television broadcasting to digital TV). These actions are of strategic importance for the European Member Countries and most candidate ones, as the DSO arises as a possible and complementary solution towards the deployment of Broadband Access Infrastructures. http://www.ist-athena.org/

AIAG, Ford, GM, NIST, Korean B2B Interoperability Testbed (KorBIT), University of Belgrade, and the EU collaborators: SAP, Italian Research Council (CNR), Gruppo Formula, Fraunhoffer Institute, and TXT Company. NIST coordinated the validation team and developed a validation framework where independently developed inventory visibility (IV) applications were harnessed to validate the ATHENA approach. In the concluding distributed validation pilot, three such IV applications, developed by GM, Ford, and University of Belgrade, successfully exchanged inventory replenishment authorization messages by relying on ATHENA developed semantic-based interoperability tools.

AIAG has worked with its industry partners and NIST to develop a standards-based approach to support cross-enterprise IV&I business processes through interoperable IV&I applications. The IV&I eKanban[24] project was adopted to be the basis for this ATHENA validation effort. Figure 4 shows the high-level architecture built for the ATHENA pilot project. The specific use case on which the team based its validation pilot was the eKanban business process. Currently, the Inventory Visibility tools are not interoperable – there are no standard global electronic eKanban visibility models nor related message sets that cover the replenishment of inventory for the automotive supply chain management. In the current standards development approaches, organizations are focusing only on normative implementation-level (rather than model-level) interoperability specification. However, one cannot adequately address semantic problems in interoperable systems in the manner that allows repeatable, testable interoperability provisioning approaches. It is necessary to identify means for tractable, precise, and accurate semantics management for data interchange standards. This issue is fundamentally a knowledge level issue although there is a strong component of Information and Communications Technology[25] as the new technologies are needed to effectively deal with this problem. This semantic management issue has been the primary technical focus of the validation pilot.[26]

---

[24] "Kanban" is a simple combination of two Japanese words—"kan," meaning "card," and "ban," meaning "signal"—that can help small and midsize manufacturers streamline their operations. Trott, Bob, "Introducing eKanban," Momentum, http://www.microsoft.com/business/momentum/content/article.aspx?contentId=760, Microsoft, 2006. e-Kanban is equivalent to an electronic card signal.

[25] http://www.cict.gov.ph/

[26] Post Test Evaluation Work package – AIAG Deliverable B5.1, Leading Partner: CRF, Security Classification: e.g., Project Participants, Version 1.0, November, 2006.

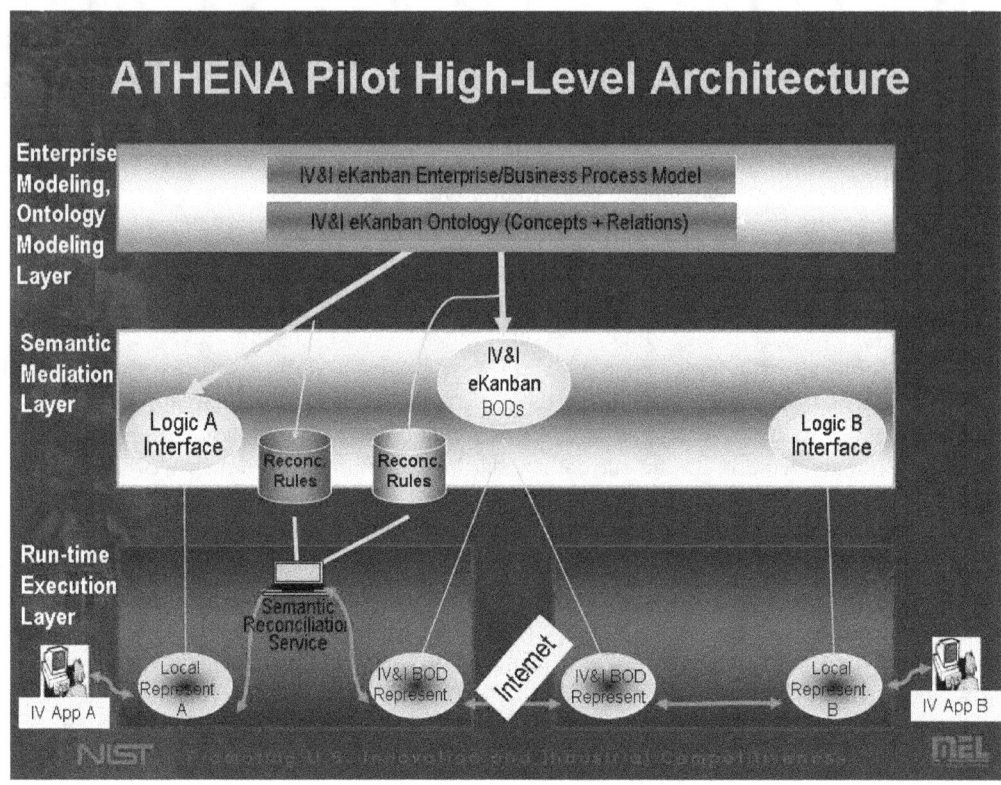

Figure 4: ATHENA Pilot Project High-Level Architecture

B2B Testbed

NIST's B2B Interoperability Testbed[27] was initiated to address the needs for demonstration and testing of business-to-business (B2B) standards in a persistent environment that provides reusability, accumulation of organizational knowledge and lessons learned, coordination, and cost-sharing among the participants. The Testbed is an on-going effort to mobilize software vendors, manufacturers, standards organizations, and other stake-holding parties to enhance the capability for on-demand demonstration and testing of interoperability of enterprise applications in a B2B setting. Its objective is to develop an open, on-going initiative to enhance the capability for on-demand interoperability demonstration and testing for use by numerous stakeholders: software vendors, manufacturing organizations (i.e., customers), standards organizations, and government. The Testbed methodology is depicted in Figure 5.

---

27 http://www mel nist.gov/msid/b2btestbed/index html

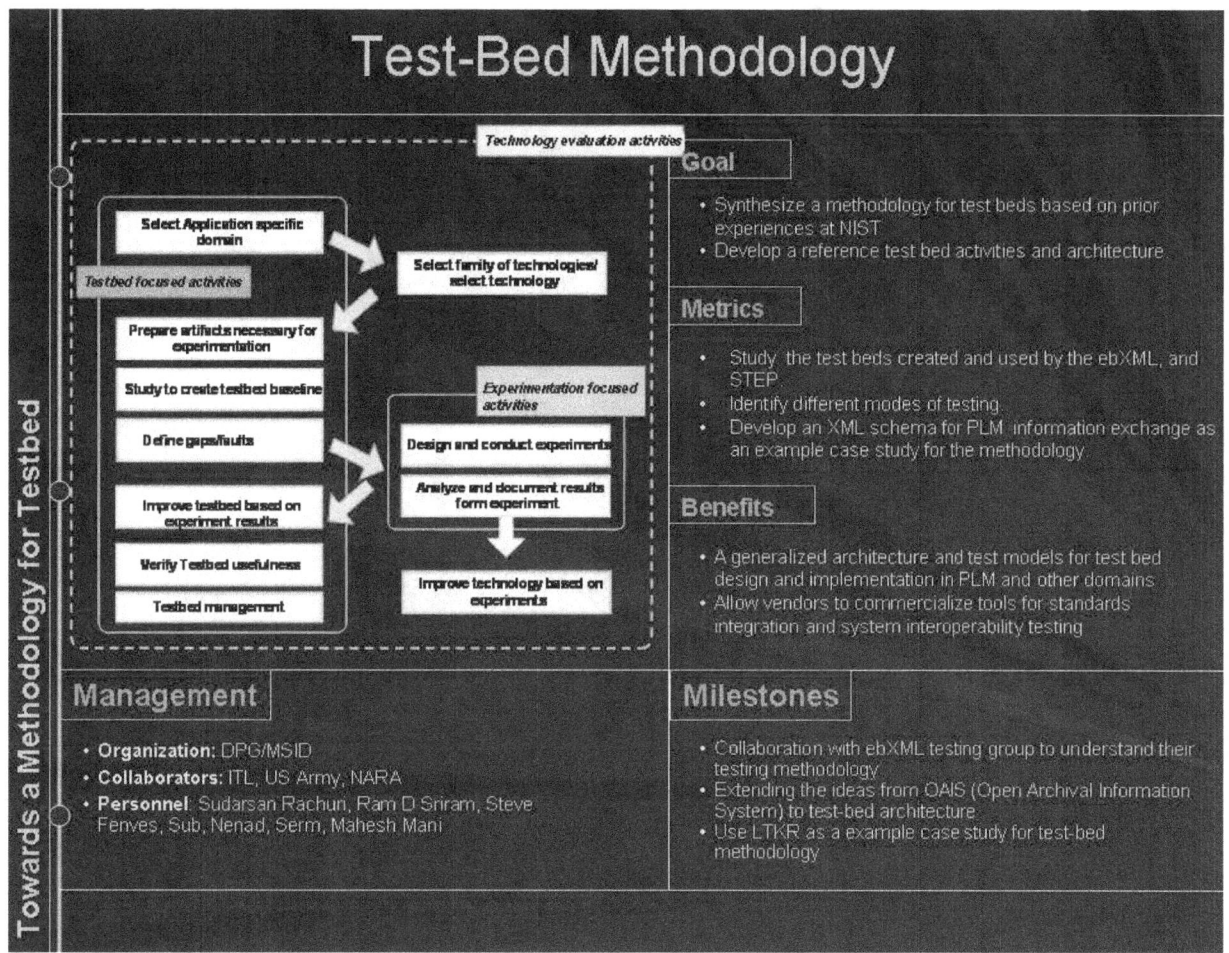

Figure 5: B2B Testbed Methodology

One of the B2B Testbed's showcase events was a demonstration of the team's Semantic and Web Services (WS) mediation for Business-to-Business integration to a group of North American automotive IT technologists and managers on November 21, 2007, in Novi, Michigan, at the First AIAG Interoperability Showcase. NIST successfully led the demonstration that exchanged messages from the University of Belgrade Faculty of Sciences (FOS) Inventory Visibility (IV) application (running in Belgrade, Serbia) and the Ford Test Harness (running in Gaithersburg, Maryland) as well as a GM IV application and the Ford Test Harness. The two independently developed applications that used different message formats and WS implementation approaches successfully used the NIST Gateway that relied on the NIST-developed eKanban ontology, the ATHENA ARGOS reconciliation rules tester/simulator, and the Johnson WS Execution Engine. The demonstration showed that the principal idea of a Semantic and WS mediator can be put in practice, and showed a running example of a first implementation of that idea. Figure 6 depicts the pilot demonstration and roles of those involved.

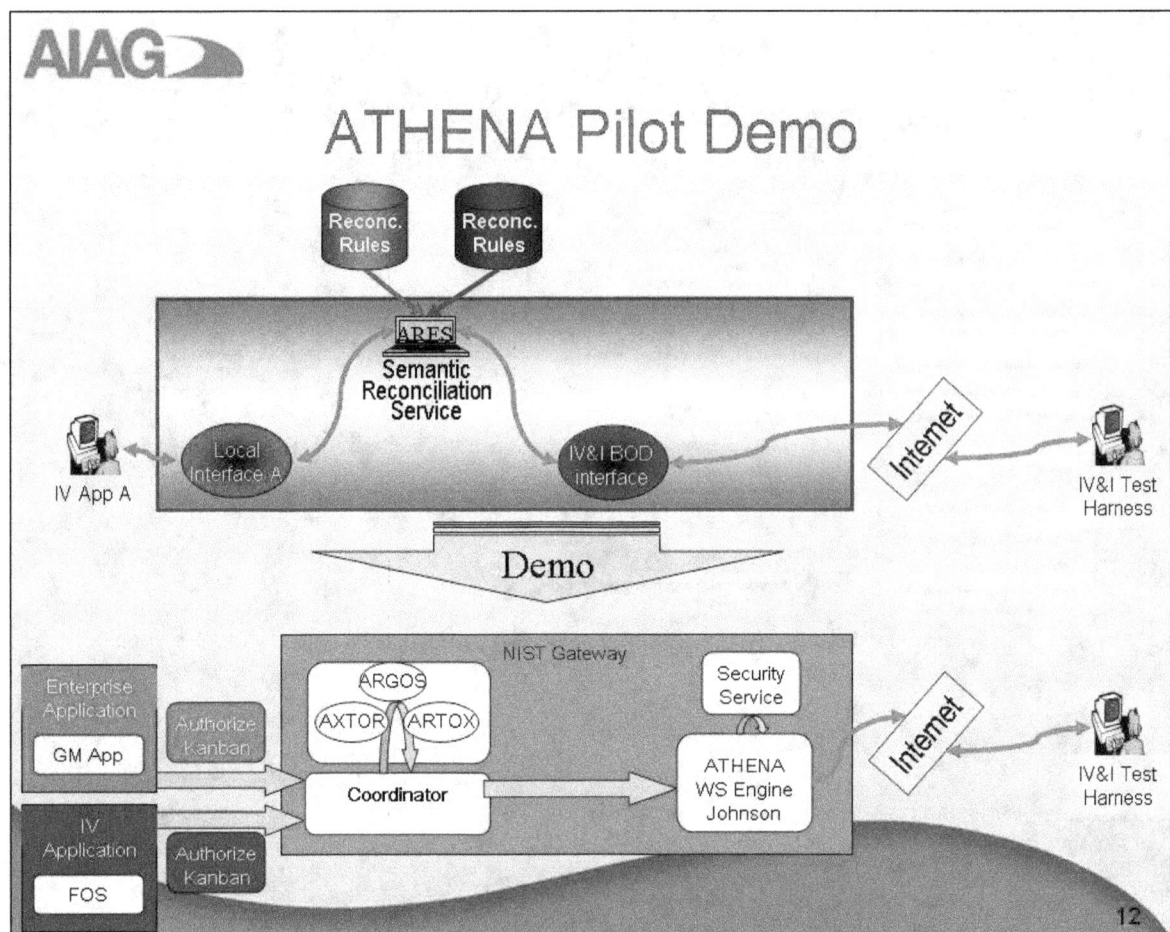

Figure 6: ATHENA Demonstration Pilot Using B2B Testbed[28]

MOSS PROJECT

The Material Off-Shore Sourcing (MOSS) project is an on-going collaboration between NIST, AIAG, Bosch, Chrysler, Ford, General Motors, Honda of America Manufacturing, and the U.S. Customs and Border Protection (CBP). The underlying hypothesis of MOSS is that there are grave deficiencies and inaccuracies in the information currently used in long distance supply chains, which adversely impact the flow of goods and the accuracy of information regarding those goods. For example, an AMR Research[29] survey reported that 15% of inbound ocean shipments experience delays in-route due to inaccurate or incomplete data. The project goals and objectives of MOSS included:

- Eliminate or significantly reduce the use of paper documents and enhance the flow of electronic information.
- Improve compliance to international standards and trade agreements.
- Improve visibility and security.
- Improve predictability and reduce trade lane uncertainty.
- Improve response to disruptions and supply chain resiliency.
- Reduce buffer inventory.
- Reduce the necessity to expedite and the inherent premium transportation costs.
- Reduce tapping personnel resources associated with manual interventions.
- Increase corporate profitability.

---

28 Ivezic, Nenad, presentation of "AIAG's ATHENA IV&I Validation Pilot" at AIAG's Interoperability Showcase, Detroit, MI, November 21, 2006.
29 http://www.amrresearch.com/

Companies historically face many failure point potentials in the request-through-delivery of goods within their supply chain. These potential failures are highlighted here in Figure 7.

Figure 7: MOSS Potential Failure Points in the Supply Chain[30]

The AMR Research survey further identified industry's pain points and found that the benefits companies expect to achieve from improvements in offshore/long distance supply chains yielded the following response:

- 78% expect reductions in buffer stock inventory.
- 74% expect reductions in the use of premium freight.
- 71% expect improved visibility to material flow.
- 61% expect improved data integrity.

The MOSS project has been working toward its objectives to fulfill the expectations that AMR Research suggested companies seek. Figure 8 shows the MOSS proof of concept to achieve these objectives.

---

[30] Presentation given on 2007-09-18 at AIAG Customs Townhall by Kevin Wade of Honda of America Mfg. and Michael Comerford of Global Commerce Systems, Inc.

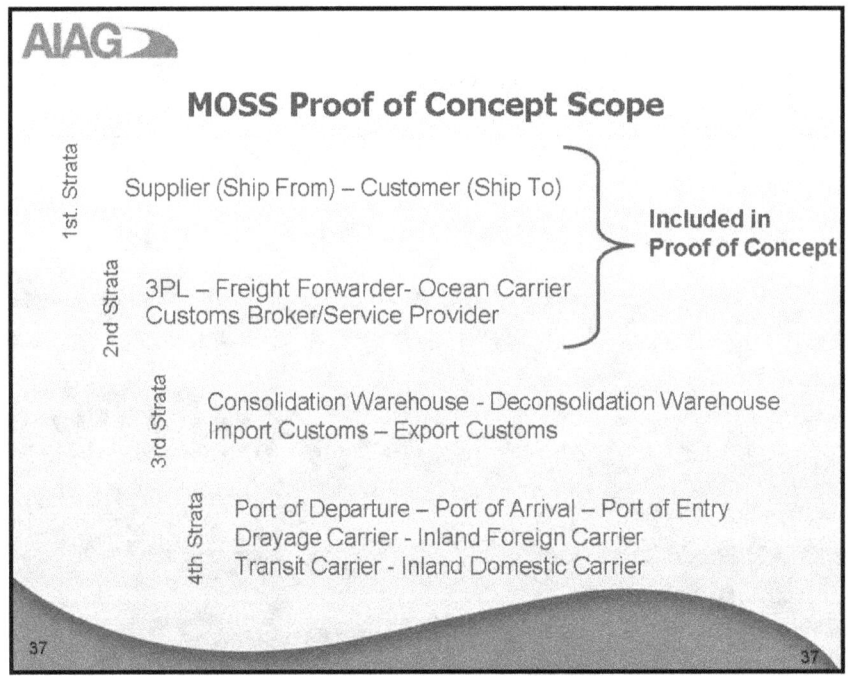

Figure 8: MOSS Proof of Concept Scope

NIST has established a testing environment for MOSS participants to carry out the scope of its proof of concept. Prior to deploying standardized solutions developed by the MOSS Project participants, the developing work needs to be validated. The testbed described in Figure 9 depicts the activities associated with the validation process of a participant's given data set. This type of testing offers real-life validation for the participant and ensures the standard develops to meet the user's requirements.

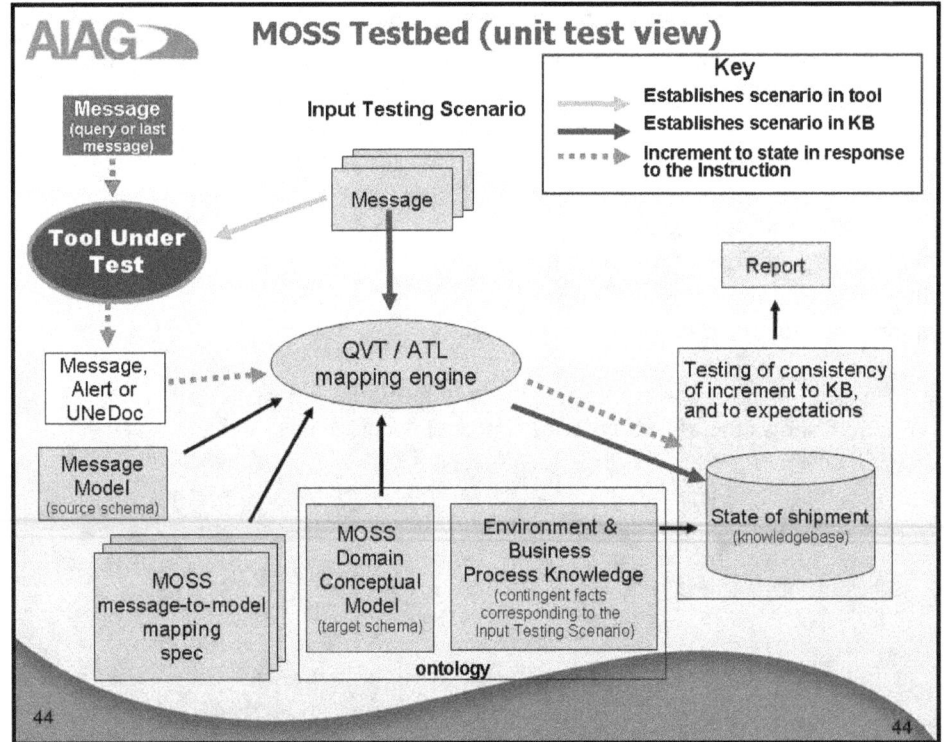

Figure 9: MOSS Testbed

While the AIAG-led MOSS project started nearer the end of the MIP, *"The MOSS viewpoint asserts that improvements in the accuracy of information conveyed—and agreement in how it is to be interpreted—will result in tangible reductions in overall supply chain transit times and measurable decreases in variation of transit times. A direct result will be reductions in buffer-stock inventory, expediting, and premium transportation costs. MOSS also seeks improvements in end-to-end shipment visibility through process and technology improvements, leading to enhanced responsiveness and resiliency. Finally, the MOSS solution, through use of emerging standards for business-to-government communications, will improve compliance and predictability to meet Customs Trade Partnership Against Terrorism (C-TPAT) and World Customs Organization (WCO) security requirements."*[31] The role of the MOSS project has only increased in priority as MIP evolves into other programs as mentioned nearer the end of this report.

METROLOGY INTEROPERABILITY TESTBED

Automotive manufacturers and suppliers lose millions of dollars and weeks of product development time from the lack of interoperability from proprietary quality data collection solutions. Currently, companies are forced to integrate data to or from numerous disparate data sources. These proprietary, integrated quality data collection solutions cost manufacturers and suppliers enormous amounts of money because of the lack of interoperability among gages and reporting tools.

The AIAG in collaboration with NIST has focused on building interface standards that solve dimensional metrology interoperability problems. The NIST Metrology Interoperability testbed allows validation of both the developing standards and the data test sets for components of dimensional metrology systems. NIST's primary tie to industry is via the AIAG Metrology Interoperability Team. Figure 10 shows the functionality of several standards of interest to this collaborative activity.

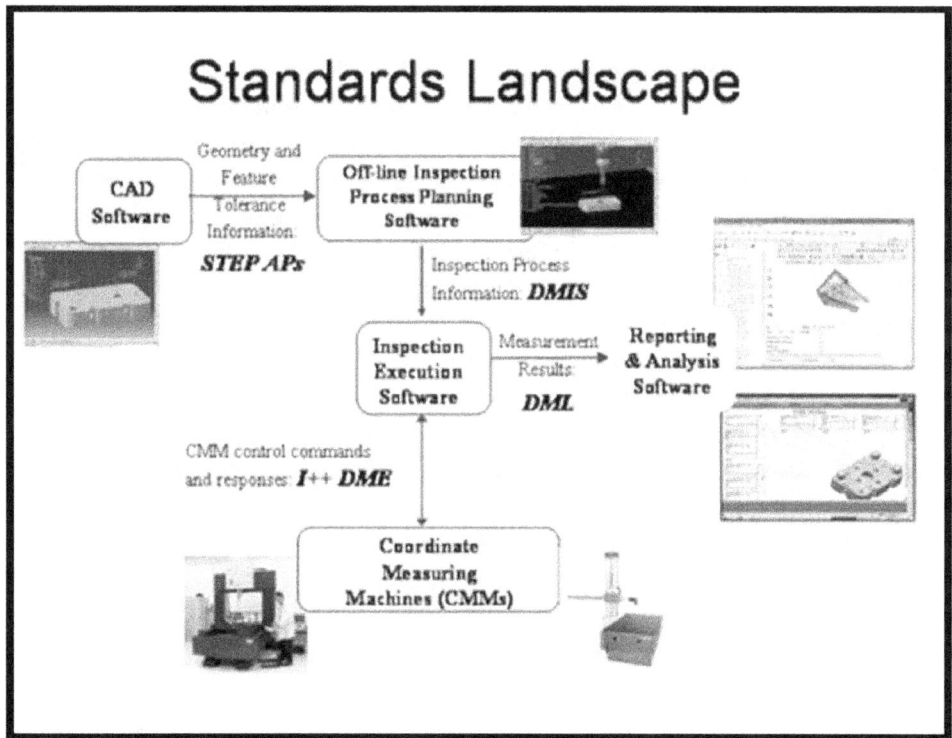

Figure 10: Dimensional Metrology Standards Landscape

---

31 Comerford, Michael and Denno, Peter, "Dealing with Data Deficiencies," Actionline, AIAG, January/February 2007.

4. Engagement with Other Government Agencies

General Services Administration

MIP testing tools and the associated MIP XML Testbed have been a collaborative project with several agencies engaged. The General Services Administration recognized early the value that NIST's MIP XML Testbed and development efforts could provide for improving interoperability across XML Schema. Its sponsorship fostered an environment for further government participation: The Data Architecture Subcommittee under the Architecture and Infrastructure Committee of the Federal Chief Information Officers Council voted unanimously to approve a new working group devoted to further development and deployment of the MIP's "Quality of Design" (QOD) XML Schema evaluation tool. This recognition resulted from successful demonstration of the QOD at numerous venues, and fruitful collaboration with stakeholders in other agencies. Plans for the working group included expanding QOD's capabilities to support not only enforcement of schema design rules and logging of test results, but also collaborative authoring and reuse of schema design guidelines across the federal government.

Internal Revenue Service

As an extension to the work funded by GSA, the Internal Revenue Service (IRS) proposed the use of MIP's XML Schema Quality of Design (QOD) tool for use in their framework as shown in **Figure 11**. QOD works with the IRS Naming Design Rules (NDR) and a Web graphic user interface to produce a schema conformance report for the user. It assists in consistently using XML Schema for the specification of information, allowing consistent design of XML schemas within an organization or single integration project, thus reducing the number and the severity of interoperability problems. Consistency makes the XML schema easier to extend, understand, implement, and maintain; and paves the way for automated testing and mapping. The IRS looks to NIST to extend QOD to better support sharing and publication of design rules with the intention of maintaining an extensive set of test cases. These extensions will allow other agencies to contribute or use published rules and test cases.

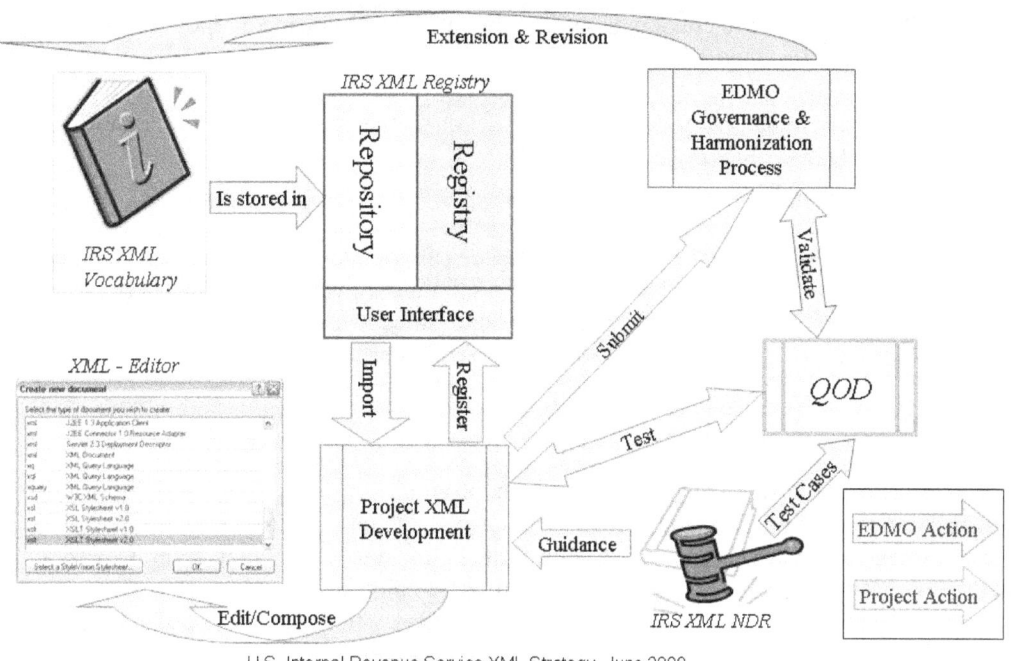

Figure 11: IRS XML Framework for Design[32]

Army

TARDEC

The need to exchange data among multiple business partners, developers, suppliers, users, and maintainers is the normal day-to-day complex business environment for the U.S. Army and other Department of Defense (DoD) Services. Product lifecycle management (PLM) is a function or a business strategy for creating, sharing, validating, and managing information about product, process, people, and services within and across the extended and networked enterprise covering the entire product lifecycle spectrum.

A number of institutions including NIST, DoD, the European Ministries of Defense and, more recently, the vendor and end-user communities have recognized the importance of interoperability across the phases and functions in PLM. A 1999 study commissioned by NIST estimated that imperfect interoperability of engineering data costs at least $1 billion per year to the members of the U.S. automotive supply chain. By far, the greatest component of these costs is the resources devoted to repairing or reentering data files that are not usable for downstream applications. This is parallel to the Army's lifecycle logistics support costs for any given weapon system and its components. As reported in a Government Accounting Office report for DoD, operating and support costs make up about 60-70 percent of a weapon system's total lifecycle costs. Since many of the current ground weapon systems will continue to be in service for another 20-30 years, the Army needs the ability to support systems after production while reducing such sustainability costs.

The PLM challenge faced by the Army is to implement standards and protocols that allow legacy systems as well as future technological innovations to interoperate seamlessly. The U.S. Army Materiel Command (AMC) is responsible for this logistics support. To achieve their goal AMC Headquarters formed the Army Product Data and Engineering Working Group (PEWG).

---

32 Triplett, John A., "IRS XML Strategy," Enterprise Data Management, IRS, June 2008.

The PEWG is chartered to provide solutions and a plan of action to address the complexities of the engineering and logistics supply chains within the Army, and to integrate these with Original Equipment Manufacturers (OEMs) and their associated enterprises that create and maintain the data in today's global business environment. As part of the PEWG, the Army Tank-Automotive Research, Development and Engineering Center (TARDEC) representative joined forces with NIST's MIP staff to collaborate on researching and producing a report in response to two milestones for PEWG's Work Package 2:

- Identify standards that could be used for lifecycle product data standardization, interoperability, and exchange among Army's and its OEMs' enterprise systems.
- Help build a business case for using standards.

The resulting report, which has received broad international distribution and discussion, was "Analysis of Standards for Lifecycle Management of Systems for U.S. Army --- a preliminary investigation."[33] There have been more than 90,000 hits to the publicly available copy on the MSID website, since its publication in August 2006, making it one of the top 10 site hits for the laboratory for publications released under the auspices of MIP.

ARMY FUTURE COMBAT SYSTEMS

Future Combat Systems (FCS) is the Army's modernization program consisting of a family of manned and unmanned systems, connected by a common network that enables the modular force providing our soldiers and leaders with leading-edge technologies and capabilities allowing them to dominate in complex environments.[34] The Model-Based Design (MBD) project is focused on integrating the engineering and manufacturing systems to allow for the elimination of shop drawings as a means of conveying design information between systems. Electronic transfer of design and manufacturing data has already increased efficiency and cut costs for certain production activities by as much as 40%.

NIST hosted the first collaborative meeting with project participants at NIST in 2006, leading a 20-member Army FCS integration development team in an analysis of ASME Y14.41[35] and its application by project participants using Pro/E Wildfire software. MIP staff worked with the Army by organizing and installing the necessary hardware and software to create a test laboratory environment at NIST for assessing MBD functionality and capability. NIST categorized requirements, restricted scope of analysis, and tracked project progress, and presented the results of this effort at FCS project meetings. Project participants were able to demonstrate issues and share best practices from their companies in a neutral environment. This effort was a critical element in the development of the Army's Model-Based Environment manufacturing architecture. Industry participants adopted new recommended practices as a result of lessons learned in this activity. NIST also worked on standards for Geometric Dimensioning and Tolerancing data representation and design release criteria to facilitate earlier release of the FCS product data to downstream activities.

Navy Chief Information Office

As an important part of its work on the development and promotion of effective data integration practices in U.S. industry and government, MSID has facilitated creating validation methodologies for World Wide Web Consortium (W3C) Extensible Markup Language (XML) Schemas.

Various entities of the federal government and others are in the process of creating guidance for organizations developing XML schemas for use within federal government organizations. Generically these types of guidance documents are referred to as "Naming and Design Rules (NDR)."

---

33 www.mel.nist.gov/msidlibrary/doc/NISTIR_7339.pdf
34 http://www.army.mil/fcs/index.html
35 American Society of Mechanical Engineers Y14.41 – 2003, "Digital Product Definition Data Practices," establishes requirements and reference documents applicable to the preparation and revision of digital product definition data, hereafter referred to as data sets.

NDRs provide guidance for developing schemas. NDRs are provided to organizations and developers in document form. The developers must interpret and develop schemas based on the verbiage included in the NDR. There is no standard mechanism or methodology currently developed that enables an organization to reliably ascertain whether a given schema conforms to the specified NDR. This, however, has not stopped the development of NDRs.

NDRs are being developed by the U.S. government as well as for foreign governments. The Navy CIO required that anyone developing schemas for the Navy shall follow these Navy NDRs rules. Specifically, under the auspices of MIP, NIST sought to define a validation for NDRs using Schematron. Schematron is a structural schema language, and is currently undergoing the International Organization for Standardization (ISO) approval (as ISO/IEC 19757 - Document Schema Definition Languages (DSDL) - Part 3: Rule-based validation – Schematron). There are many different NDRs that could be used to define this validation, but MIP staff expressly chose those defined by the U.S. Navy to comply with joint requirements and to achieve a common structure and language for information handling. As the Navy CIO viewed XML as a key enabler of the Department's net-centric data strategy, NDRs were expected to facilitate the discovery and use of common data across the naval enterprise. The Navy felt that using the NDRs would move the DoN forward to ensure that all XML is based on a consistent set of schemas through the application of open standards. The Schematron schema was tested on valid schemas developed by NIST and based on the Navy NDR. XSLT[36] was used as the testing platform for the schema.[37]

MIP staff were instrumental in coding the Navy's NDRs to Schematron. The results of NIST's work:

- Took the Navy NDRs and made them enforceable.
- Objectively and systematically analyzed the Navy NDR specification.
- Provided recommendations for tighter language to expressly link producability to the OASIS[38] Universal Business Language.

DoD Systems Software & Engineering Office

On 29 November 1994, the Honorable Paul G. Kaminski, Under Secretary of Defense for Acquisition and Technology, directed Acquisition Executives in the Department of Defense to use "open systems" specifications and standards (electrical, mechanical, thermal) for acquisition of all weapon systems electronics to the greatest extent practical.

The Open Systems Joint Task Force (OSJTF) was formed in September 1994 to "Sponsor and accelerate the adoption of open systems in weapons systems and subsystems electronics to reduce life-cycle cost and facilitate effective weapon system intra- and interoperability."[39]

MIP staff completed the development of the EXPRESS Injector software to support the OSJTF efforts as part of our sponsorship and collaborative relationship with OSJTF. The EXPRESS Injector produces an XML file conforming to the OMG XMI (XML Metadata Interchange) language and the EXPRESS meta-model defined as part of the OMG MEXICO project. Tools were also developed for validation and conformance testing of SysML and UML. These tools are being used as part of the ungoing SysML Plug Fest sponsored by NIST and OSJTF.[40]

---

36 Extensible Stylesheet Language Transformations, http://www.w3.org/TR/xslt
37 The Navy NDR is the product of expertise and energies contributed by representatives from 13 key Navy, Marine Corps, and Secretary of the Navy organizations who participated in the DON XML Working Group. To ensure these rules are applicable and current, the DON Chief Information Officer (DON CIO) established the XML Business Standards Council and proceeded to charter the Net-Centric Technical Standards Council to serve as liaison to organizations developing national and international standards for XML and Web Services technologies. All commands in the Navy and Marine Corps that are developing systems that use XML, in accordance with the DON XML Policy, are expected to apply these standards to maximize interoperability and enable a net-centric environment for enhancing supportability of operations across the Department. Wennergren, D. M., DoN/CIO memorandum of 18 January 2005, "Extensible Markup Language (XML) Naming and Design Rules Official Release."
38 Organization for the Advancement of Structured Information Standards, http://www.oasis-open.org/home/index.php
39 http://www.acq.osd.mil/osjtf/overview.html
40 http://syseng.nist.gov/se-interop

The Plug Fest, co-hosted by NIST and DoD OSJTF, provides an environment for Software Engineering (SE) tool developers to assess the interoperability of their implementations. Interoperability among SE tools is essential to the development of complex systems and system-of-systems (SoS) analysis. Such work often involves the collaboration of many disparate organizations. This work environment usually does not permit organizations to standardize on a single SE tool, and often not even on the same standard (e.g., SysML™). The Plug Fest will provide an environment for evaluating the interoperability of tools within the context of a single exchange standard, and across standards.

Since the purpose of the Plug Fest is to foster tool interoperability, the primary focus is the exchange of SE data among tools that implement standardized SE data interfaces. Initially, interfaces supported within the scope of the Plug Fest will include selected model interchange aspects of the following specifications:

- OMG's SysML XMI
- ISO 10303-233
- ISO 10303-21

The Plug Fest is designed as a series of "challenge problems" or "exercises" shown in Figure 12 that are intended to allow participants to assess the interoperability of their tools.

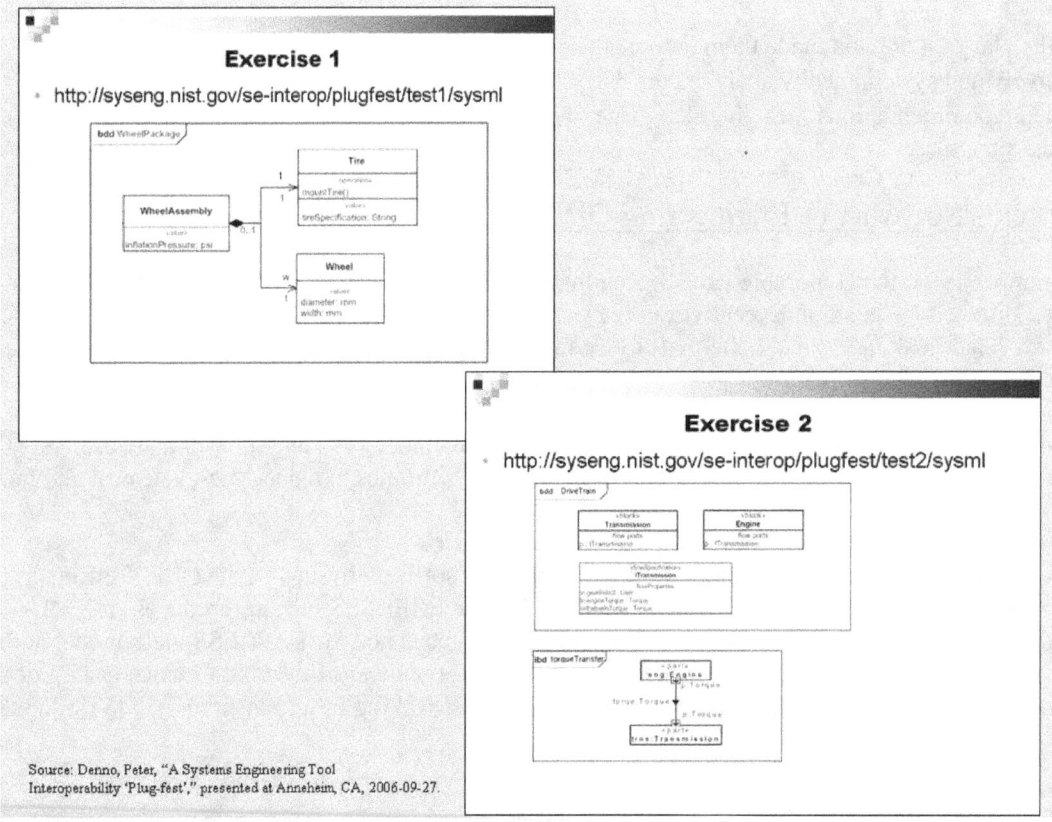

Figure 12: Examples of Plug Fest Exercises

The NIST UML/SysML Validator[41] performs conformance testing, as a prerequisite to the interoperability testing that is the central concern of the Plug Fest. In the Plug Fest process, only exchange files that do well on the conformance criteria will be allowed to be uploaded into the common area and shared with other participants. Figure 13 shows a screenshot of the Validator, as well as a sample of the type of violations that might be reported as a result of running one's implementation through the Validator.

---

41 http://syseng.nist.gov/se-interop/plugfest/tools

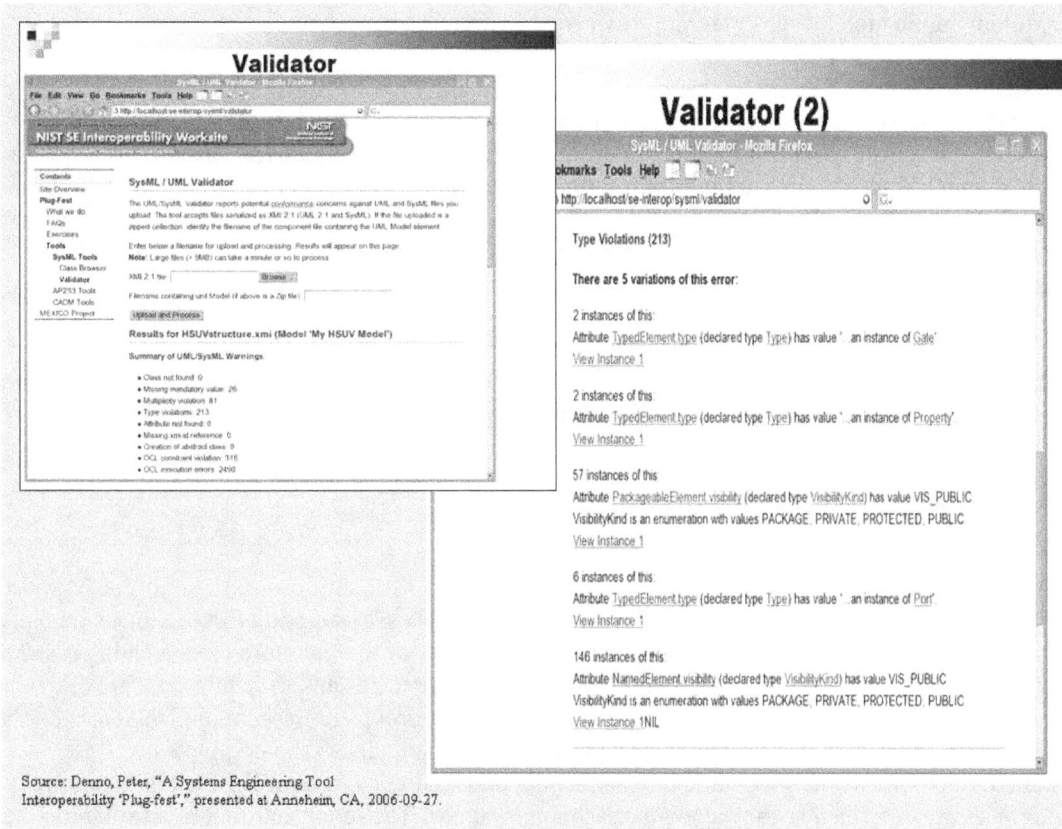

Figure 13: Validator Used in Plug Fest

UN/CEFACT

The United Nations Centre for Trade Facitiliation and Electronic Business (UN/CEFACT) is a United Nations body created to encourage close collaboration between governments and private businesses to secure the interoperability for the exchange of information between the public and private sector.[42] UN/CEFACT is one of the collaborative bodies working hand-in-hand with MIP's B2B Testbed. This Testbed is discussed in more detail below.

5. Results and Impact

This section highlights the many contributions made by the MIP staff over the three years of the Program's existence. First it focuses on the research results from our examination of semantic technologies and information modeling evolution for manufacturing. Next, highlights our technical leadership in standards development and resulting impacts for interoperability solutions. Finally, our work to progress conforming implementations through our test tool development and testing services has accelerated both the development of standards' solutions and provided implementers a means to ensure compliance to published information technology documentary standards.

Semantic Research Contributions

AMIS

One of the critical research projects for MIP was to investigate the state of the art for semantic application that could be applied to improve interoperability. The Automated Methods for Integrating Systems (AMIS) project

---

42 http://www.unece.org/cefact/about.htm

evaluated the options for systems integration using today's technology as well as what would be necessary to achieve maximum automation by self-integrating systems[43], a concept for the future.

The initial objective of the AMIS project was to reduce the cost and time for software integration by devising methods, algorithms, and tools by which activities of a systems engineer could be automated. The motivation for this work was to reduce the expense of integration efforts where traditional standards-based approaches were inappropriate or ineffective, e.g., where the time it takes to develop a standard is longer than the life of the integration problem. The anticipated benefits of this project included improved interface and service specifications, improved knowledge capture for existing software systems and standards, and reduced time and cost of systems integration projects. In addition, this work helped to identify the unsolved problems, and provide knowledge for new toolkits.

The AMIS approach was based on the idea that the published interface specifications for a software system could be abstracted into an understanding of the roles in the business processes the system was built to support. Those roles could be formalized into specifications and models for interactions in which each element would be associated with the corresponding business action/entity/property notion.

REASONERS

Under the sponsorship of the U.S. National Security Agency (NSA), MIP staff provided an in-depth report summarizing their work on the foundation for reasoning system metrics, to support NSA's choices in applying automated reasoning to homeland security. Staff conducted a review of the literature on evaluating reasoning systems, identified critical aspects of modern logic programming languages and semantics that are relevant to security analysis, and published a report of our findings. The report groups representation languages by their relation to first-order logic, and model-theoretic properties, such as soundness and completeness. Inference procedures are divided into deduction, induction, abduction, and analogical reasoning. Capabilities of user and software interfaces are described as they apply to reasoning systems. The report introduces information metrology, model theory, and inference to facilitate understanding of the reasoning categories presented. It concludes with recommendations for future work.[44] This effort helped establish NIST's reputation internationally, as experts on first-order logic, reasoners, and semantic technologies.

Information Models

Data communication among heterogeneous systems is always a concern, particularly in situations where the support of a universal data exchange standard is unavailable. Many integration projects today rely on shared semantic models based on standards represented using XML technologies. An information model is a representation of concepts, relationships, constraints, rules, and operations to specify data semantics for a chosen domain of discourse. It is important for effective information sharing and integration. The advantage of using an information model is that it can provide shareable, stable, and an organized structure of information requirements for the domain context. It serves as a medium for transferring data among computer systems that have some degree of compliance with this information model.

INFORMATION MODEL FOR MACHINE SHOP

A machine shop information model was developed by MIP staff as part of the efforts to support the developing standard data interfaces. The machine shop information model is used for representing and exchanging machine shop data, initially among manufacturing execution, scheduling, and simulation systems. Staff also developed a software architecture, standard data interfaces, and a prototype generic machine shop simulator that can be readily reconfigured for use by a large number of small machine shops. The architecture for the generic machine shop simulator is divided into the following component elements: neutral shop data file, XML data processor, system supervisor and reporting, machine shop emulator, discrete event simulator, and a user interface system. The

---

43 http://www mel nist.gov/publications/view_pub.cgi?pub_id=822162
44 Bock, C, Gruninger, Michael, Libes, Don , Lubell, Joshua , Subrahmanian, Eswaran, *Evaluating Reasoning Systems*, NISTIR 7310, (2006), www nist.gov/msidlibrary/doc/NISTIR_7310.pdf

machine shop information model is a key factor in effectively and efficiently integrating the generic machine shop simulator. Figure 14 illustrates some of the major elements of the conceptual information model and their relationships to each other.

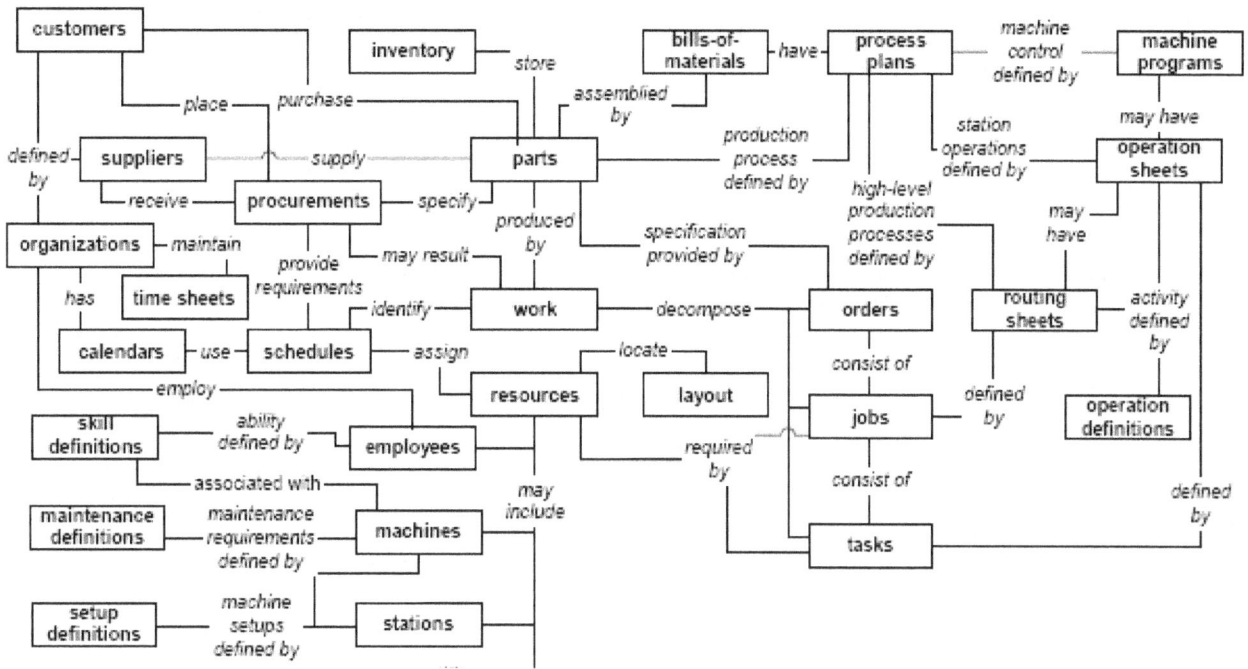

Figure 14: Concept for the Machine Shop Information Model

INFORMATION MODEL FOR PRODUCT REPRESENTATION

Prior to the Manufacturing Interoperability Program commencing, NIST staff developed the initial concepts and model for product representation known as the Core Product Model (CPM). Under the Program work plan this model and the Open Assembly Model (OAM) continued to be enhanced and fine-tuned to best meet industry's needs. The CPM provides a base-level product model that is not tied to any vendor software; is open, non-proprietary, simple, generic, expandable, independent of any one product development process; and capable of capturing the engineering context that is shared throughout the product lifecycle. The CPM's product lifecycle management support better ensures reliable, complete, and efficient data models.

The OAM represents the function, form, and behavior of assemblies and defines both a system level conceptual model and the associated hierarchical relationships. The model provides a way for supporting tolerance representation and propagation, representation of kinematics, and engineering analysis at the system level.

The development of the OAM is geared towards overcoming the interoperability issues between different CAD tools during different phases of an assembly design. The main difference of the OAM from any other available standard is that the assembly model created is not at the end of the product design; instead, the model evolves from an incomplete, preliminary form to a complete model as the design progresses from early design to detailed design phases. Initially, the model starts with customer specified functions and functional requirements. On completion of the design, the OAM databases contain detailed information regarding function, behavior, form/structure, kinematics, assembly and tolerance information for the entire product.[45] NIST continues to enhance the CPM,

---

45 Rachuri, Sudarsan, et al, "Information Models For Product Representation: Core And Assembly Models," NISTIR 7173, December 2004.

further the development of the OAM, and move them forward for formalized standardization in international standards development organizations.

Standards Development and Enhancements

Over the course of MIP, several standards development and enhancement efforts were underway. MIP staff often played key technical leadership or facilitator roles in driving the standards to completion, and ensuring the standard met the requirements for those vested industrial and government partners. The following highlights those standards initiatives where we had a notable role in its development.

SYSTEMS MODELING LANGUAGE (SYSML)

Systems engineering is a discipline aimed at reliably producing high-level designs of hardware, software, or manual systems from requirements. The Systems Modeling Language (SysML) standardized by the Object Management Group (OMG), is a graphical modeling language for specifying, analyzing, designing, and verifying complex manufactured systems that may include hardware, software, information, personnel, procedures, and facilities. In particular, the language provides graphical representations with a semantic foundation for modeling system requirements, behavior, structure, and parametrics, which is used to integrate with other engineering analysis models. See Figure 15.

SysML uses the OMG XML Metadata Interchange (XMI) to exchange modeling data between tools, and is also intended to be compatible with the evolving ISO 10303-233 systems engineering data interchange standard. The inter-relationships between ISO/CD 10303-233 and SysML is depicted in Figure 16.

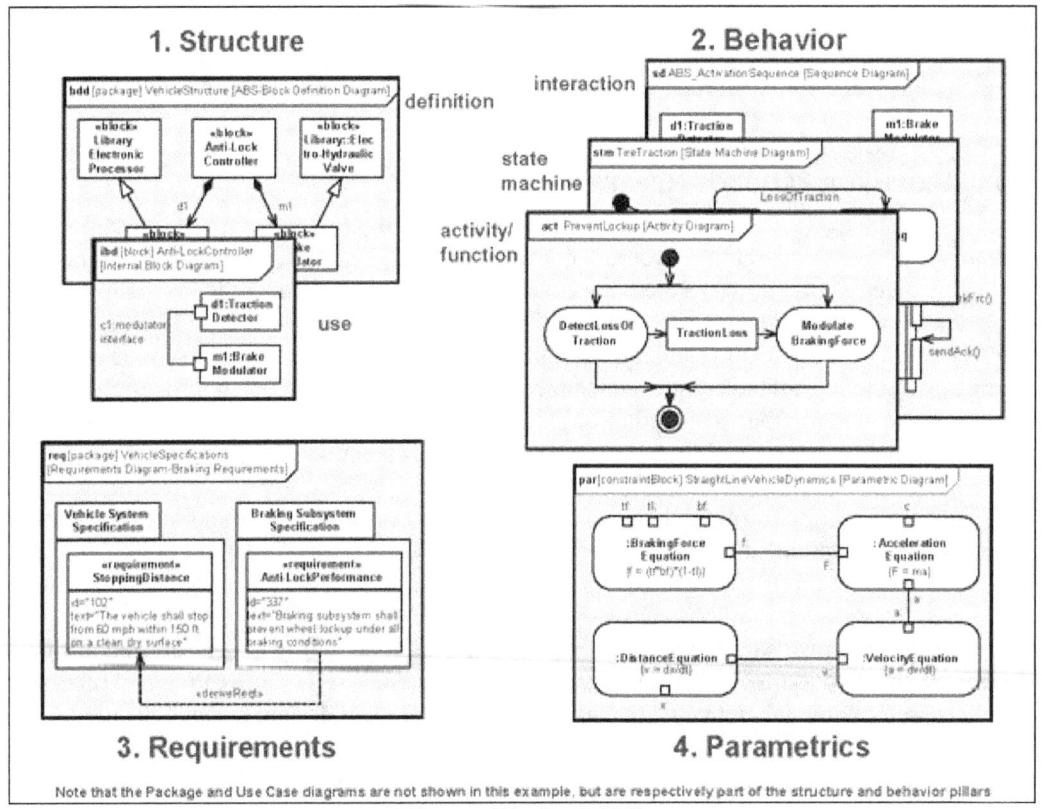

Figure 15: SysML[46]

---

46 http://www.omgsysml.org/

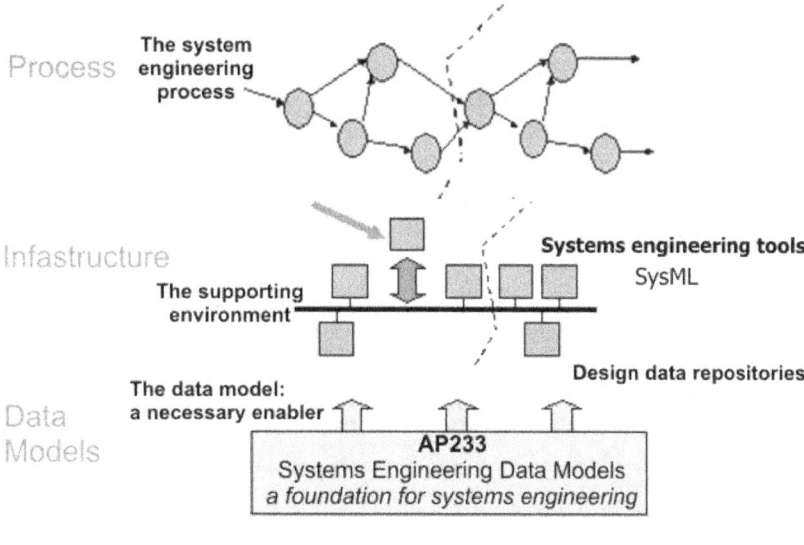

Figure 16: SysML and STEP[47]

SysML was adopted by the Object Management Group, with major contributions from NIST's MIP staff. Contributions were in the critical area of process modeling, and in cooperation and liaison with the International Council on Systems Engineering48. The standard took many years to develop, and now that it is a standard, is already implemented by several systems modeling companies, and is used in the development of large-scale products in the military and industry.

ONTOLOGY DEFINITION METAMODEL (ODM)

Under the auspices of MIP, NIST managed the entire four-year development cycle of the Ontology Definition Metamodel (ODM) — from conception to adoption by OMG. In addition to this leadership, NIST was also a principal technical contributor to the effort, which involved four software providers and other experts throughout the world. The result of this multi-year effort was the international standardization of ODM. The standard supports four existing international standard knowledge representation languages, bringing them together in a common modeling framework. This represents the foundation for an important set of enabling capabilities for Model Driven Architecture-based software engineering, namely the formal grounding for representation, management, interoperability, and application of business semantics. ODM is applicable to knowledge representation, conceptual modeling, formal nomenclature development, and ontology definition; and enables the use of a variety of enterprise models as starting points for ontology development through mappings to other languages. Reasoning tools can be used to reconcile the terms found in various forms of electronic business transactions, enabling manufacturers to communicate reliably with new software suppliers. With ODM, such communication will not require developing partner-specific translation software, which introduces longer lead times, human errors, and inhibits innovative partnerships. Benefactors of ODM other than the manufacturing community — notably the intelligence community, the emergency response community, and the healthcare community who are actively involved in the development, use and exchange of ontologies.

---

47 http://www.ap233.org/
48 http://www.incose.org/

UNIFIED MODELING LANGUAGE (UML)

NIST led the introduction of process modeling in the Unified Modeling Language (UML), the globally dominant and information modeling standard in use today. UML models application structure, behavior, and architecture, as well as manufacturing process and structure. Beginning with UML 2.0 (published in November 2007[49]), the UML Specification was split into two complimentary specifications: Infrastructure and Superstructure. The UML infrastructure specification defines the foundational language constructs required for UML 2.1.2. It is complemented by UML Superstructure, which defines the user level constructs required for UML 2.1.2. The two complementary specifications constitute a complete specification for the UML 2 modeling language.

It has been a catalyst for the evolution of model-driven technologies, which include model-driven development (MDD), model-driven engineering (MDE), and model-driven architecture (MDA). By establishing an industry consensus on a graphic notation to represent common concepts like classes, components, generalization, aggregation, and behaviors, UML has allowed software developers to concentrate more on design and architecture. Dozens of analysis and design tools built on UML are on the market today.

META-OBJECT FACILITY (MOF)

MOF is an OMG standard for model-driven engineering. MOF is designed as a four-layered architecture. It provides a meta-meta model at the top layer, called the M3 layer. This M3-model is the language used by MOF to build metamodels, called M2-models. The most prominent example of a Layer 2 MOF model is the UML metamodel, the model that describes the UML itself. These M2-models describe elements of the M1-layer, and thus M1-models. These would be, for example, models written in UML. The last layer is the M0-layer or data layer. It is used to describe real-world objects.[50]

The MOF Specification is the foundation of OMG's industry-standard environment where models can be exported from one application, imported into another, transported across a network, stored in a repository and then retrieved, rendered into different formats (including XMI, OMG's XML-based standard format for model transmission and storage), transformed, and used to generate application code. NIST led the development of a MOF 2.0 metamodel for EXPRESS, ISO 10303-11[51]. Under the MIP initiatives, we also developed an EXPRESS injector, a tool that maps EXPRESS schemas to the EXPRESS meta-model, producing the XML Metadata Interchange (XMI).[52]

BUSINESS PROCESS MODELING NOTATION (BPMN)

MIP provided the leading expert on the OMG Finalization Task Force. This Task Force performs the first maintenance revision on the specification, resolving issues submitted to OMG, while simultaneously producing implementation back in their companies. BPMN provides a standard visualization mechanism for business processes defined in an execution optimized business process language. BPMN will provide businesses with the capability of understanding their internal business procedures in a graphical notation and will give organizations the ability to communicate these procedures in a standard manner. The specification was first published in January 2008, and as of that same month, there were already 44 implementations of BPMN.[53]

---

49 http://www.omg.org/spec/UML/2.1.2/
50 http://en.wikipedia.org/wiki/Meta-Object_Facility
51 ISO 10303-11:2004, Industrial automation systems and integration -- Product data representation and exchange -- Part 11: Description methods: The EXPRESS language reference manual, Edition 2.
52 http://www.omg.org/spec/XMI/2.1.1/
53 http://www.bpmn.org/

BUSINESS MOTIVATION MODEL (BMM)

OMG's BMM specification provides a scheme or structure for developing, communicating, and managing business plans in an organized manner. Specifically, BMM does all of the following:

- It identifies factors that motivate the establishing of business plans.
- It identifies and defines the elements of business plans.
- It indicates how all these factors and elements inter-relate.

Among these elements are those that provide governance for and guidance to the business — Business Policies and Business Rules. NIST provided a participating expert on the OMG Finalization Task Force for developing the Business Motivation Model. The initial specification was approved and published in September 2007, and provides a scheme or structure for developing, communicating, and managing business plans in an organized manner.

SEMANTICS OF BUSINESS VOCABULARY AND BUSINESS RULES (SBVR)

OMG's SBVR defines the semantics of business vocabulary, business facts, and business rules; as well as an XMI schema for the interchange of business vocabularies and business rules among organizations and between software tools. NIST supported this standardization effort with a principal technical expert who worked to resolve harmonization for the specification. The initial standard was published in January 2008.

BUSINESS PROCESS DEFINITION METAMODEL (BPDM)

As of the publication of this report, OMG's BPDM was adopted by OMG, and Version 1.0 available. BPDM provides the capability to represent and model business processes independent of notation or methodology, thus bringing these different approaches together into a cohesive capability. This is done using a meta model – a model of how to describe business processes – a kind of shared vocabulary of process with well defined connections between terms and concepts. This meta model captures the meaning behind the notations and technologies in a way that can help integrate them and leverage existing assets and new designs. The meta model behind BPDM uses the OMG "Meta Object Facility" (MOF) standard to capture business processes in this very general way and to provide an XML syntax for storing and transferring business process models between tools and infrastructures. Various tools, methods and technologies can then map their way to view, understand and implement processes to and through BPDM Execution-interoperable process models can execute the same way for all parties interchanging the model. NIST introduced execution interoperability for the first time in an adopted process model, using advanced metamodeling techniques to ensure compatibility with ISO 18629, the Process Specification Language.

PROCESS SPECIFICATION LANGUAGE (PSL)

International Organization for Standardization's (ISO) Process Specification Language defines a neutral representation for manufacturing processes that supports automated reasoning. Process data is used throughout the life cycle of a product, from early indications of manufacturing process flagged during design, through process planning, validation, production scheduling and control. PSL has had its first application to conventional manufacturing process languages, improving the efficiency and reliability of system construction. It resulted in the first standardized process model designed from the ground up with PSL's precision in mind, in collaboration with OMG. MIP staff received testimonials from major corporations in appreciation of its leadership and technical achievements in this area (e.g., Boeing, Borland, Unisys, Electronic Data Systems, Lombardi, and General Services Administration). The PSL standard is a fully axiomatized, first-order logic ontology to support the unambiguous description and exchange of process information. NIST provided the initial draft specifications and technical leadership in having the first 8 parts of ISO 18629 published as International Standards.

OWL WEB ONTOLOGY LANGUAGE (OWL)

Developed by the World Wide Web Consortium (W3C), OWL is designed for use by applications that need to process the content of information instead of just presenting information to humans. OWL facilitates greater machine interpretability of Web content than that supported by other standards, and by providing additional vocabulary along with a formal semantics. OWL has three increasingly-expressive sublanguages: OWL Lite, OWL Description Language, and OWL Full.

The Semantic Web is a vision for the future of the Web in which information is given explicit meaning, making it easier for machines to automatically process and integrate information available on the Web. The Semantic Web will build on XML's ability to define customized tagging schemes and RDF's flexible approach to representing data. The first level above RDF required for the Semantic Web is an ontology language what can formally describe the meaning of terminology used in Web documents. If machines are expected to perform useful reasoning tasks on these documents, the language must go beyond the basic semantics of Resource Description Framework (RDF) Schema. OWL has been designed to meet this need for a Web Ontology Language. OWL is part of the growing stack of W3C recommendations related to the Semantic Web.

In comparison to the XML and RDF standards, OWL adds more vocabulary for describing properties and classes. XML provides a surface syntax for structured documents, but imposes no semantic constraints on the meaning of these documents. XML Schema is a language for restricting the structure of XML documents and also extends XML with datatypes. RDF is a datamodel for objects ("resources") and relations between them, provides a simple semantics for this datamodel, and these datamodels can be represented in an XML syntax. RDF Schema is a vocabulary for describing properties and classes of RDF resources, with a semantics for generalization-hierarchies of such properties and classes.[54]

NIST staff developed the first extension of OWL, which enabled specification of complex assembled products and automated design checking. We developed the extension and guided implementation and proof-of-concept construction.

SEMANTIC WEB SERVICES LANGUAGE (SWSL)

SWSL is a logic-based language for specifying formal characterizations of Web service concepts and descriptions of individual services. It includes two sublanguages: SWSL-FOL — a full first-order logic language, which is used to specify the Semantic Web Services Ontology (SWSO), and SWSL-Rules — a rule-based sublanguage, which can be used both as a specification and an implementation language. As a language, SWSL is domain-independent and does not include any constructs specific to services. SWSL includes two separate sublanguages, because W3C developers believe that different tasks associated with Semantic Web services are better served by different knowledge representation formalisms.

SWSL-Rules is a rule-based language with non-monotonic semantics. It is designed to provide support for a variety of tasks that range from service profile specification to service discovery, contracting, policy specification, and so on. The language is layered to make it easier to learn and to simplify the use of its various parts for specialized tasks that do not require the full expressive power of SWSL-Rules.

SWSL-FOL describes a methodology for translating SWSL-FOL specifications into SWSL-Rules with "minimal loss." This means that inferences made using the translated specification are sound with respect to the original SWSL-FOL specification, and the "lost" inferences (i.e., formulas that are derivable from the original but not from the translated specification) are, in some sense, minimized. It is used to specify the dynamic properties of services, namely, the processes that they are intended to carry out.[55]

---

54 http://www.w3.org/TR/owl-features/
55 http://www.w3.org/Submission/2005/SUBM-SWSF-SWSL-20050909/

NIST was part of the member submission team for proposing SWSL formally to W3C, and continues to play a key role in its development and enhancements.

QUALITY MEASUREMENT DATA (QMD)

The QMD Specification enables the seamless exchange of quality measurement information between disparate and proprietary gauges and reporting tools and solves this data integration problem by reducing as many as 1,500 data formats to one single open reporting format. The QMD specification is the work of the AIAG Metrology Project Team (MEPT)Quality Measurement (MEQM) working group. The goal of the MEQM has been to produce a non-proprietary, computer-readable, and widely implemented standard for the interface between measurement devices (not merely dimensional) and Statistical Process Control (SPC) analysis software packages. The QMD standard holds promise to save the U.S. SPC software industry alone around $50 million over the next few years.

NIST has actively collaborated with AIAG's MEPT to support the QMD specification with test suites that provide a development tool to an implementer of the QMD specification, enabling the implementer to quickly, correctly, and completely generate an implementation of QMD. Using the NIST QMD test suite will also allow end users and tier suppliers to easily perform their own tests on QMD implementation files to verify vendor claims of compliance to QMD prior to software purchase or payment of software licensing fees. The NIST QMD test suite was recognized as a great asset to partnering vendors to validate their QMD implementations prior to demonstrating data exchange at the Quality Expo held in Chicago in 2007.

DIMENSIONAL MEASUREMENT INTERFACE STANDARD (DMIS)

DMIS is being developed by the Dimensional Metrology Standards Consortium and ISO (as ISO 22093). Figure 17 shows the dimensional measurement equipment world before DMIS, and the effects of DMIS on that world today. The DMIS standard provides interoperability standards for coordinate measurement machines. NIST has contributed significantly to the standard and produced a suite of conformance testing tools. The DMIS specification is currently written and read by nearly every Coordinate Measuring Machine (CMM) software vendor worldwide. However, proprietary languages and a variety of incompatible non-complaint DMIS implementations still abound. Because of this, NIST is working to ensure a persistent testing and evaluation service is in place. NIST is providing the first set of tools with which vendors and users can evaluate and ensure the conformance of a particular implementation to the DMIS specification.

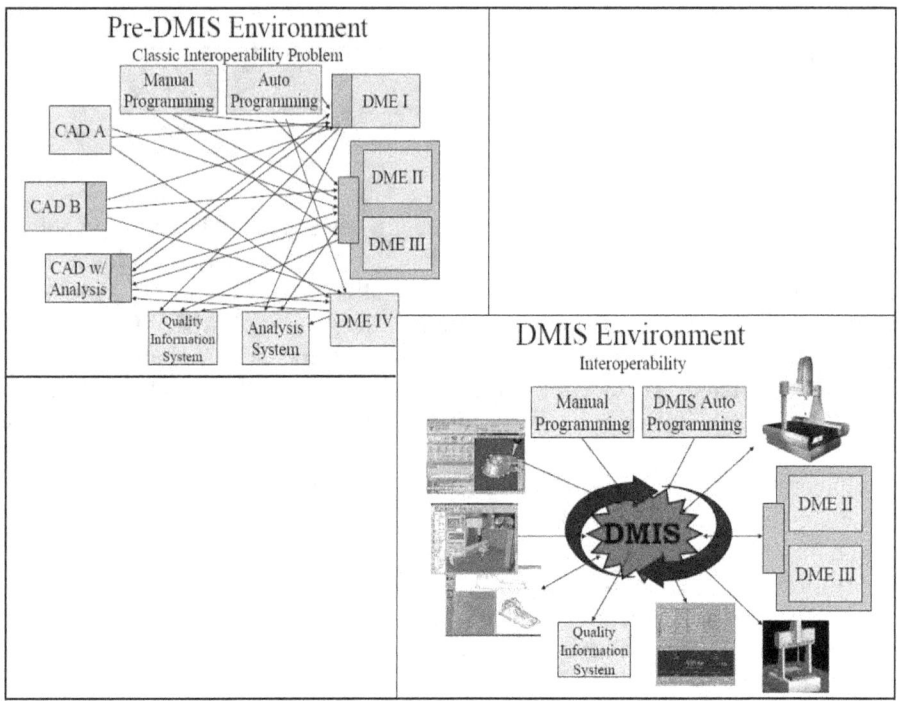

Figure 17: The Impact of DMIS[56]

INSPECTION PLUS-PLUS (I++) DIMENSIONAL MEASUREMENT EQUIPMENT (DME) STANDARD

The standards development organization for I++ is actually a community of interest known as International Association of Coordinate-Measuring-Machine-Manufacturers[57]. Founded in 1999, the group is comprised of seven automotive manufacturers (Audi, BMW, DaimlerChrysler, Opel, Porsche, Volvo, VW) with a common goal to describe the need of car manufacturers for new concepts for a general definition of the complete measuring process.[58] The I++ standard provides interoperability standards for coordinate measurement machines. The standards' landscape for dimensional metrology is depicted in Figure 18.

NIST has contributed significantly to the standard and produced a suite of conformance testing tools. As like DMIS, the I++ DME standard[59] is currently written and read by nearly every CMM hardware and software vendor worldwide. Incompatible, non-compliant I++ DME implementations are rare due to the influence of NIST's early and active participation in the standards development process.

---

56 Stone, Robert J., "DMIS – A Data Exchange Protocol for Dimensional Measurement," presentation at International Metrology Interoperability Summit, NIST, Gaithesburg, MD, March 2006.
57 International Association of Coordinate-Measuring-Machine-Manufacturers is not an official SDO, although this has become a defacto international standard.
58 Resch, Josef, "Portrait I++," presentation at International Metrology Interoperability Summit, NIST, Gaithesburg, MD, March 2006.
59 http://www.iacmm.org/media/pdf/gen/c96e69c2fe2a41eb83b199858126903c.pdf

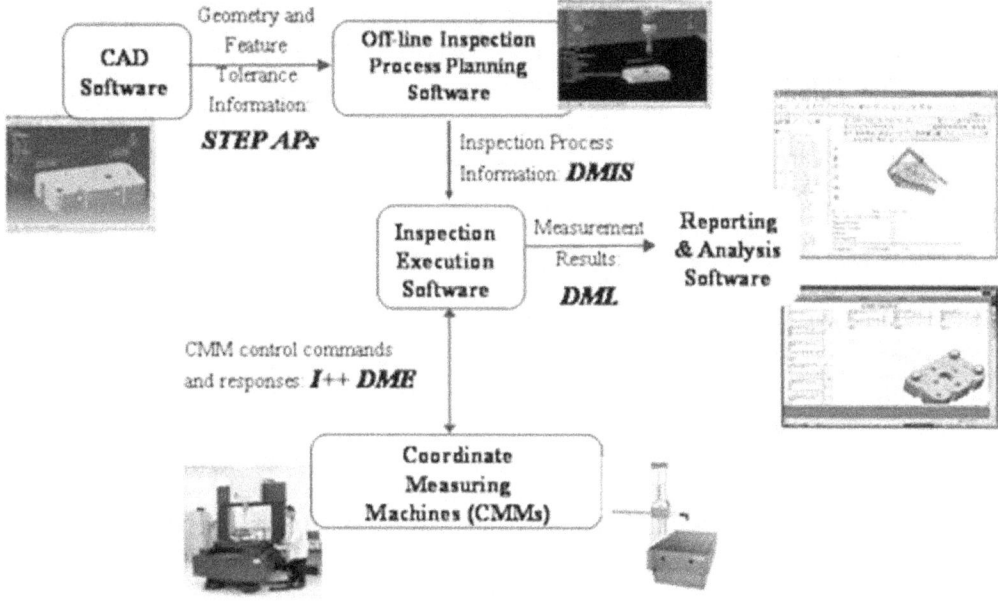

Figure 18: Dimensional Metrology Standards Landscape

CORE MANUFACTURING SIMULATION DATA (CMSD) SPECIFICATION

CMSD defines a data interface for efficient exchange of manufacturing life cycle data for integrating manufacturing software applications with simulation systems. A multi-year effort by NIST staff resulted in the initial draft and the continued technical leadership of the evolving CMSD specification. The Simulation Interoperability Standards Organization (SISO) is leading the standardization effort. The initial effort has focussed on machine shop data definitions, and the plan is to extend the data specification to include supply chain, aerospace assembly operations, automotive vehicle assembly operations, plant layout, and other relevant manufacturing and simulation information.

This standardization effort is to promote the increased, widespread, and pervasive use of advanced manufacturing technologies, in particular, the simulation technology in the manufacturing industries. Volvo Car Company has historically conducted discrete event manufacturing simulation without benefit of a standard specification. From this experience, simulation engineers at the company recognized 3 basic deficiencies: 1) manufacturing simulation model development takes too long and costs too much, 2) manual data input for simulation models is error prone, takes too much time, and increases costs, and 3) interoperability is lacking between simulation systems and manufacturing applications. Volvo, Chalmers University, and NIST collaborated in a case study to integrate CMSD with a Volvo paint shop process operation to explore the benefits of using a standardized simulation data specification. This case study demonstrated the viability of using the CMSD specification to address the issues.

An implementation study of the CMSD information model for a Volvo Truck engine-line simulation was also completed. The study included the development of a data converter, interface tool, and simulation model. The data converter translates data from specific factory shop-floor databases at Volvo Trucks into a CMSD-structured XML file. The data included in the databases cover product variants, workstation cycle time, and logged breakdown data. The interface tool is for generic and integrated CMSD interfaces to enable use of CMSD XML files as data sources for the UGS Plant Simulation software. To further demonstrate the viability of the CMSD specification for other simulation software, a second CMSD interface, based on the same principles as the first, was developed for the Enterprise Dynamics simulation software, using the same CMSD XML file.

The impact of these case studies with Volvo resulted in:

- Viewing the SISO CMSD specification as an enabling technology for manufacturing data exchange by Volvo, and a practical and innovative method for simulation model construction.
- Reducing costs for multiple simulation runs by automatically exchanging manufacturing data as input to the simulation model.
- Promoting the use of standard specifications to exchange manufacturing data between manufacturing applications and simulation systems.

STANDARD FOR THE EXCHANGE OF PRODUCT MODEL DATA (STEP) STANDARDS

ISO 10303, Industrial automation systems and integration standards, informally known as STEP --- STandard for the Exchange of Product model data, has been an ongoing international standardization effort since the early 1980s. Several of the STEP specification development efforts led by MIP staff or sponsored by NIST, advanced or came to fruition during the Program's duration:

- ISO 10303-108[60] specifies the resource constructs for the representation of model parameters and constraints in CAD or other kinds of models, together with the mechanisms necessary for associating them with geometric or other elements of transferred models. The use of these capabilities potentially allows certain aspects of the behavior of a model in its originating system to be conveyed together with the basic model itself. The intention in transferring this additional information is to provide the receiving system with data that will enable it to reconstruct corresponding behavioral characteristics in the model following the transfer. Ideally, this will enable the model to be edited in the receiving system just as though it had been created there. That would not be possible without the exchange of what is known as design intent information. ISO 10303-108 enables the capture and transfer of an important aspect of design intent.
- ISO/TS 10303-203[61] specifies the application protocol for configuration controlled three-dimensional design of parts and assemblies. The following are within the scope of ISO/TS 10303-203:
    - Products that are three dimensional mechanical parts and assemblies.
    - Product definition data and configuration control data pertaining to the design phase of a product's development.
    - Representation of an instance of a part in an assembly through its usage in a sub-assembly.
    - Six groups of shape representations of a part that include advanced boundary representation, faceted boundary representation, manifold surfaces with topology, geometrically bounded surface and wireframe geometry, wireframe with topology, and constructive solid geometry in three-dimensions.
    - Geometric validation properties to allow the translation of geometric shape representations (advanced boundary representation and faceted boundary representation solids) to be checked for quality.
    - Geometric presentation of geometric shape representations by the application of colors, layers and groups.
    - Geometric and dimensional tolerances applied to geometric shape representations.
    - Textual annotation and notes applied to geometric shape representations.
- ISO 10303-111[62] represents shape elements available in modern CAD systems in a manner suitable for use in procedural or construction history modeling.

---

[60] ISO 10303-108:2005, Industrial automation systems and integration -- Product data representation and exchange -- Part 108: Integrated application resource: Parameterization and constraints for explicit geometric product models.
[61] ISO/TS 10303-203:2005, Industrial automation systems and integration -- Product data representation and exchange -- Part 203: Application protocol: Configuration controlled 3D design of mechanical parts and assemblies (modular version).
[62] ISO 10303-111:2007, Industrial automation systems and integration -- Product data representation and exchange -- Part 111: Integrated application resource: Elements for the procedural modeling of solid shapes.

Testing & Evaluation Support

To support the validation of content standards or exchange specifications, NIST has defined a process known as the Model Development Life Cycle. Our experience has shown that this process is a logical process used by people developing content standards supporting data exchange. The process is independent of how the exchange is physically manifested, e.g., whether they use XML or some other means of data sharing. The process seems to be consistently followed whether the project explicitly intends to follow it or not. By recognizing the process up front, projects are able to streamline their efforts and thus save time and aggravation, speed up the delivery of the content standard, and improve the overall quality of the final result.

As industry standards are increasingly built with flexibility to support users in various industrial sectors such as automotive, healthcare, formal semantics and structure requirements have been placed into separate layers of specification and some are delayed until the standard implementation. In addition, most popular schema languages do not provide sufficient expressiveness to support accurate and precise semantic expression.

An extensively sophisticated schema specification will be too complex a specification for implementers to effectively use. A simplistic schema specification, on the other hand, will be too loose and will allow for imprecise specifications. Nevertheless, the separation of lexicons, structures, and semantics of a content specification into layers positively affects the adoption of the standard.

The work NIST has been doing provides an infrastructure to enable the exchange of manufacturing and business data, support for testing and validating manufacturing and business specifications, and provides public tools for the use of XML Schema used in systems integration. These tools support schema development, testing, deployment, and management.

The following briefly describes the tools that have been developed under the auspices of MIP, and many are available on our MSID website via: http://www.mel.nist.gov/msid/XML_testbed .

Business Process Monitor - The Business Process Monitor takes Business Process Specification Schema (BPSS) and Collaboration Protocol Agreement (CPA) instances as input and produces a graphical presentation of the collaboration as an output. The monitoring tool is implemented as a Java applet, which enables it to run in web browsers.

Content Checker - The Content Checker tool assists in the consist application of XML Schema specifications to real business transactions. It allows one to write, store, and execute rules against which instance data is validated. Many content standards are emerging today based on XML Schema. These specifications define semantics and structure for data to be exchanged between systems. However, in the interest of creating reusable standards, the specifications often do not capture the full range of semantics which will be needed in individual transactions. This tool is especially useful in the scenario where standardized data exchange specifications are used but the transaction restricts the data in ways that are not specified. The restrictions can be codified using the tool and the data can be validated against those restrictions.[63]

The Content Checker seeks to complement this structure by providing a facility to precisely specify, extend, and test for conformance data being exchanged based on the semantics defined in an XML schema, or content standard.

Naming Report - The Naming Report will generate a list of terms used to construct names for types, elements, and attributes within a schema. Names are divided into terms based upon Camel Case conventions. For example, a complex type with the name "ShipToAddress" will be broken up into the terms "Ship," "To, and "Address." Generating this list of terms may help developers recognize inconsistent or invalid terms. The Naming Assister is a more comprehensive tool NIST has developed to support this effort.

---

[63] Morris, KC; Goyal, Puja; Frechette, Simon, "Development Life Cycle and Tools for Data Exchange Specification," Proceedings of the ASME 2008 International Design Engineering Technical Conference & Computers and Information Engineering Conference (IDETC/CIE 2008), Brooklyn, NY, August 2008.

Naming Assister - Providing a consistent naming convention for elements and types is essential in the creation, development, and maintenance of XML schemas. It improves schema readability and consistency, consequently speeding up future schema adoptions and implementations. The Naming Assister specifically aids in creating consistent compound names by verifying the construction of these names against a table of allowable terms.[64] It focuses on mapping terms used to assemble element or type names against a table of allowable terms, and checking the construction of compound names to ISO-11179[65] recommended naming convention. This tool was originally written to determine naming inconsistencies within particular Testbeds XML schemas, and to assist in the establishment of a table of standard terms.

NIST XML Schema Validation Service - Schema validation is a web-based service that allows the user to upload their own schema file, or a zip file containing multiple schemas, and validate it against the W3C standard specification for XML schemas. If a zip file is uploaded, the user must specify the target schema file name in order for the tool to know where to begin validation.

NIST Instance Validation Service - Instance validation is a web-based service that allows the user to upload their own XML instance and validate its content with either their own uploaded schema, or from three publicly available schemas:

- OASIS Universal Business Language v1.0
- Grants.gov v1.0
- OAGIS v9.0

Note that instance validation is one way to validate that an XML schema meets the requirements captured in an XML schema. If errors are encountered during instance validation, it may reflect problems in the XML schema.

Schematron Editor Tool - The objective of the Schematron Editor tool is to provide a Java-based graphical user interface tool for business analysts to easily create, view, and modify Schematron files. The tool includes a number of wizards to facilitate specification of constraints without requiring expertise in XML Path Language (XPATH)[66] and Extensible Stylesheet Language Transformation (XSLT)[67] syntaxes. The tool also provides the ability to test an XML instance file against the constraints defined by the current Schematron file. The tool can also be extended to work in conjunction with XML Schemas for validating an instance.

Quality of Design (QOD) - The XML Schema Quality of Design Tool (also called the QOD Tool) provides a repository of rules and a framework to publish and execute design rules. It assists in consistently using XML Schema for the specification of information. Consistent design of XML schemas within an organization or single integration project can reduce the number and the severity of interoperability problems. In addition, this consistency makes the XML schema easier to extend, understand, implement, and maintain; and, it paves the way for automated testing and mapping. Applying best practices is one way to achieve this design consistency.

The purpose of QOD is to provide a prototypical environment for checking the XML schema design quality in a collaborative environment. QOD is intended for those developing guidelines for writing high quality XML schemas and those actually writing XML schemas. The tool allows users to create their own requirements or select their own set of requirements against which to check XML schemas.[68] Figure 19 shows the QOD testing environment NIST has in place today. Figure 20 shows our plans to extend the QOD testing environment to include an NDR authoring and sharing environment.

---

64 Ibid
65 ISO/IEC 11179: 2004, Information technology – Metadata registries
66 http://www.w3.org/TR/xpath
67 http://www.w3.org/Style/XSL/
68 Morris, KC et al, "Development Life Cycle and Tools for Data Exchange Specification."

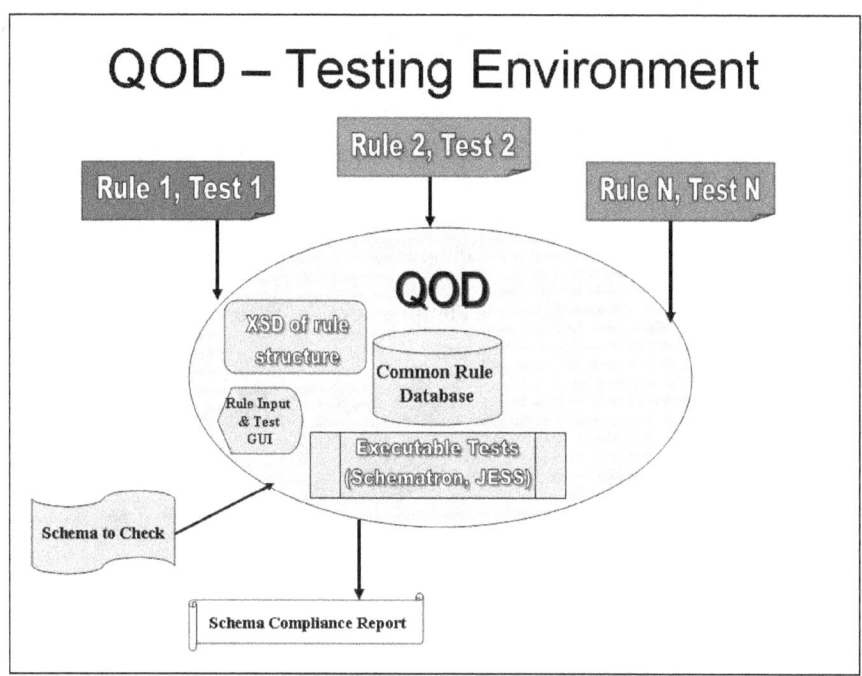

Figure 19: QOD Testing Environment

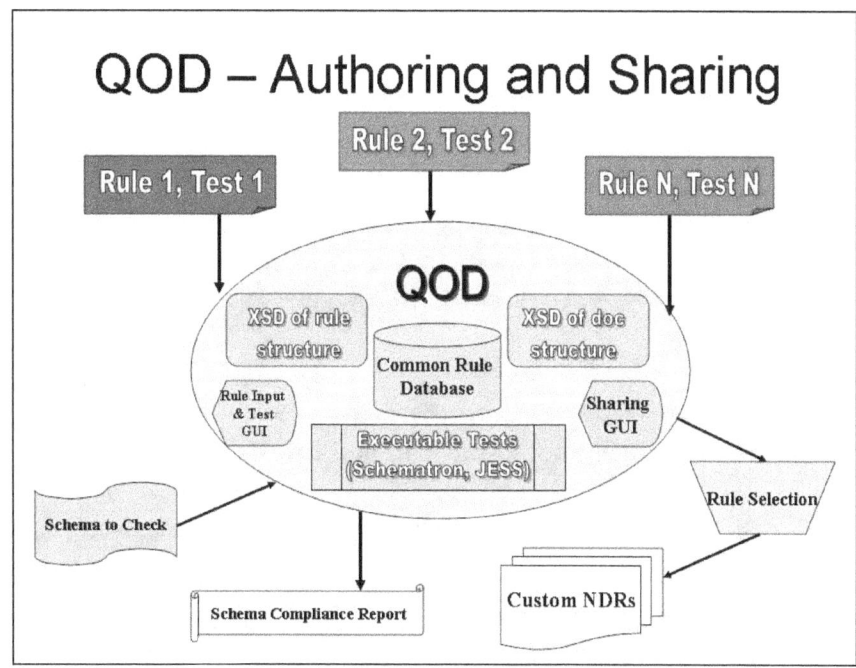

Figure 20: QOD Authoring and Sharing Environment

As of this publication, the QOD contains test profiles for several NDR specifications, and custom profiles can be created as well. These NDR specifications include those for the Department of Navy, the Internal Revenue Service, several for UBL and OAGi, as well as coverage for the UN/CEFACT NDR.

Information Mapping Test Tool - The Information Mapping Test Tool assists in verifying the implementation of XML import and export functions. The goal of this tool is to accelerate development of these features for a variety of software. NIST is currently looking for collaborators who would be interested in working with us to further develop this tool by providing user feedback on the tool as it currently exists.

Semantic Technology Support Software

MINIMAL INTERFACE TO VAMPIRE (MIV) - MIV (Minimal Interface to Vampire) provides a graphical user interface to the open source version (version 2) of the Vampire Theorem Prover. The interface provides the user with the ability to load KIF (Knowledge Interchange Fomat) or SUO-KIF (Standard Upper Ontology-Knowledge Interachange Format) axioms and present problems to Vampire for evaluation. The system provides formatted presentation of the proof generated by Vampire (See Figure 21).

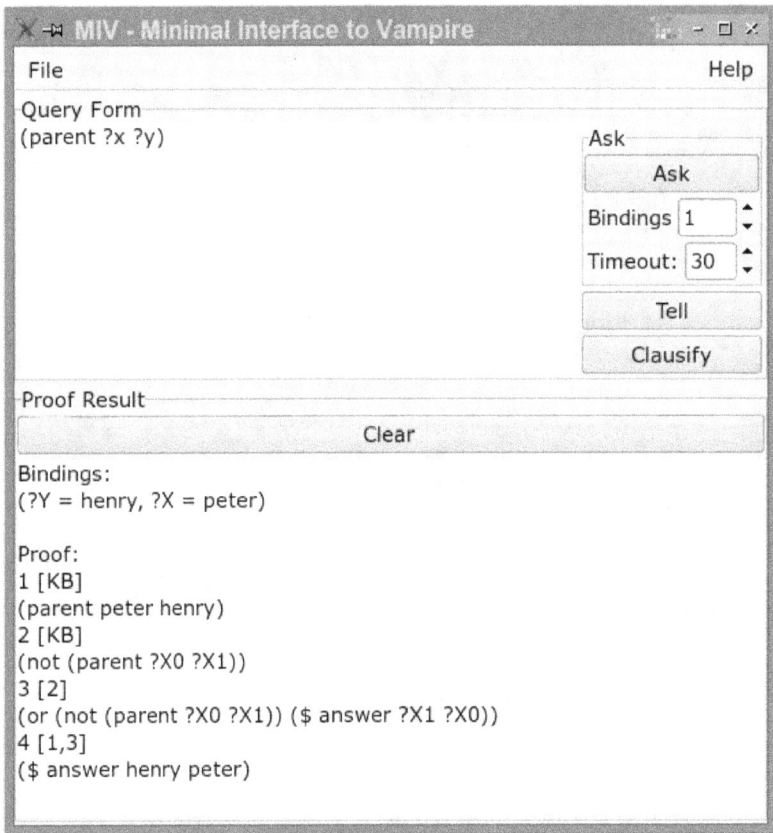

Figure 21: Screen Shot of the Minimal Interface to Vampire

PSL'S "20 QUESTIONS" – PSL's 20 Questions is a tool to help map process characteristics into PSL Ontology concepts.

SUMO2LOOM NIST has developed Sumo2loom software, that has been transferred and made publicly available at Teknowledge Corporation and announced to the Loom user community. This NIST transfer drew the attention of several respected researchers, including Loom maintainer Thomas Russ, (who wrote, "Wow, this is great!"). SUMO (Suggested Upper Merged Ontology) is an ontology being created as part of the Institute of Electrical and Electronics Engineers, Inc. (IEEE) Standard Upper Ontology Working Group. The goal of this Working Group is to develop a standard upper ontology that will promote data interoperability, information search and retrieval, automated inferencing, and natural language processing.

Loom is a knowledge representation language developed by researchers in the Artificial Intelligence research group at the University of Southern California's Information Sciences Institute. NIST's translating program, SUMO2LOOM, was developed to translate SUMO into a form that can be used by the LOOM-V4 inference engine. Loom has been distributed to more than 80 universities and corporations, and is being used in numerous Defense Advanced Research Projects Agency (DARPA)-sponsored projects in planning, software engineering, and intelligent integration of information. Having a program that will translate the IEEE SUMO to LOOM will reach a large LOOM-user community, enhance the adoption of SUMO, an improve interoperability among users.

Application Support Software

AUTOMATING EQUIPMENT INFORMATION EXCHANGE (AEX) SCHEMAS- FIATECH is a consortium that provides global leadership in identifying and accelerating the development, demonstration and deployment of fully integrated and automated technologies to deliver the highest business value throughout the life cycle of all types of capital projects. The FIATECH AEX Project provided XML schemas for capital facilities equipment and associated documentation. NIST built software and test suites for the AEX XML schemas supporting capital facility equipment engineering, procurement, construction, and operations and maintenance work processes.

EXPRESS INJECTOR - The EXPRESS Injector is a tool that maps EXPRESS schemas (ISO 10303 Part 11 form) to OMG's XMI, using the EXPRESS meta-model.

EXPRESSO FOR LINUX AND WINDOWS – Expresso (a sample output shown in Figure 22) is a tool to aid in the development and validation of EXPRESS schema. It also provides an Express-X mapping engine.

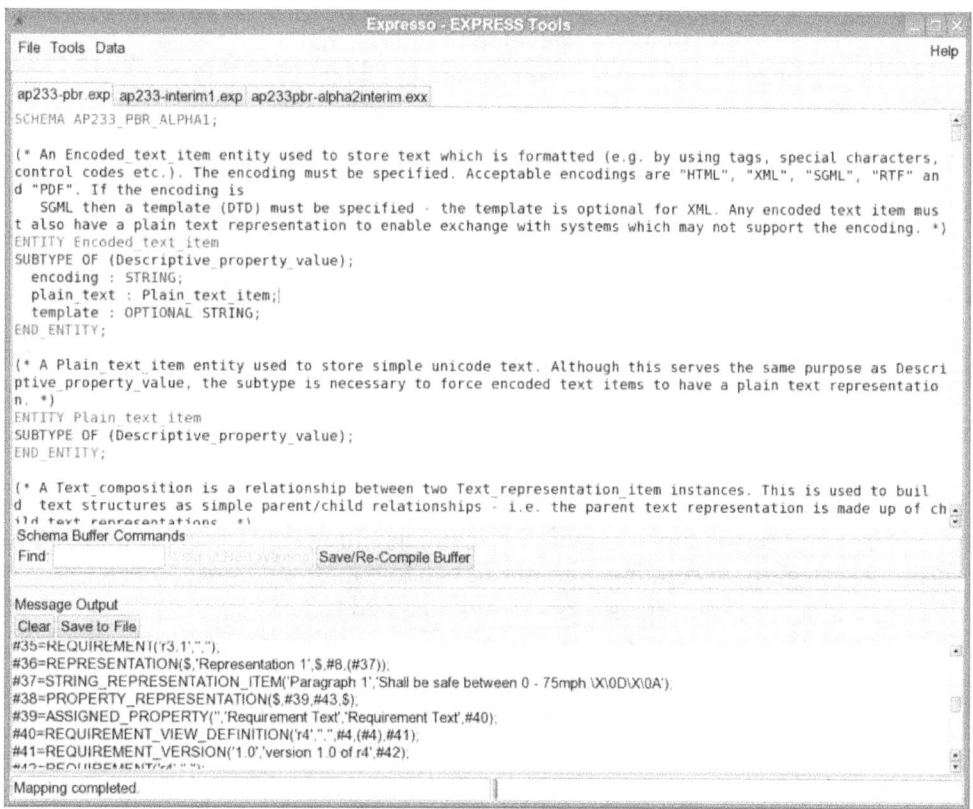

Figure 22: Expresso Example

Manufacturing Simulation Models

A set of manufacturing simulation models have been developed to:

- Demonstrate system integration, business processes, and manufacturing operations.
- Validate manufacturing plans, data, and numerical control programs.
- Evaluate business and manufacturing strategies.

Audio Video Interleaved (AVI) files are provided as samples of some of the work NIST has done in the area of simulation and visualization for manufacturing. The following table provides a brief summary of the types of AVI files we have developed. The downloadable files are available at http://www.mel.nist.gov/msid/avi_downloads.html .

MODEL	OBJECTIVE	FUNCTIONALITY	SYSTEM	DOWNLOAD
Shop Floor Layout	Develop solutions for engineering tool integration	Develop interfaces and demonstrate the integration of engineering tools with manufacturing shop floor and machine tool simulators to validate manufacturing plans, programs, and data.	Delmia Igrip	sfl.zip (5.5 MB)
Virtual Machining of a Boeing Part	Develop solutions for engineering tool integration	Develop a virtual NC machine model is developed to validate the operation plan and NC programs.	Delmia VNC	boeing.zip (1.7 MB)
Virtual Makino Machine	Develop solutions for engineering tool integration, creating models of machines and their operations	Develop a virtual Makino high-speed machining center to validate the operation plan and NC programs.	Delmia VNC	makino.zip (4.8 MB)
Simulation of a Computer Manufacturing Supply Chain	Model Defense Department supply chains	Develop supply chain simulation models and templates to evaluate different coordination strategies for manufacturing supply chains.	Extend	cmsc.zip (2.4 MB)
Shipbuilding Simulation	Develop generic model templates and data interfaces for the	Develop a shipyard simulation model to demonstrate shipbuilding	ProModel	shipyard.zip (1.7 MB)

MODEL	OBJECTIVE	FUNCTIONALITY	SYSTEM	DOWNLOAD
	simulation of the fabrication and assembly processes associated with shipyard block construction	resource allocation strategy.		
Black & Decker Drill Assembly Line	Working with industry to develop engineering solutions	Identify simulation modeling and data interface requirements for modeling manual manufacturing assembly lines.	Delmia Quest, Igrip	bdda.zip (42.1 MB)
Black & Decker Miter Saw Assembly Line	Working with industry to develop engineering solutions for Production System Engineering	Develop activity models and data interfaces for the design, engineering, and simulation of manufacturing systems.	Delmia Igrip	bdaa.zip (53.3 MB)
HLA-Based Distributed Simulation	Establish standard interfaces and conformance tests for simulation to support the construction of distributed simulation systems based upon High Level Architecture (HLA) technologies	Develop interfaces and mechanisms for integrating Commercial Off-the-Shelf manufacturing simulation software to meet the needs of globally distributed enterprise modeling in various enterprise domains; integrating commercial simulation tools using HLA.	ProModel, ARENA	ds_2.zip (75.3 MB)

Spreading the Word

Besides effectively spreading the word through our demonstrations and persistent testing environments for staging real-life applications collaboratively with industry, another means of disseminating has been through the reputation of the high-quality staff we employ for our work, through our technical leadership, publishing our research results (see the section on References at the end of this report), and hosting relevant workshops.

MIP-RELATED WORKSHOP HIGHLIGHTS

One of the ways we are able to take the pulse of other government agencies, industry, and academia is through planning and hosting workshops on topics key to resolving manufacturing interoperability problems. Provided in reverse chronological order, the workshops where we played a prominent role are highlighted here.

Interoperability Week, 2008
NIST's third annual Interoperability Week was held at Gaithersburg, MD, April 28-30, 2008. The Interoperability Week conference provided a venue for people from different disciplines to compare issues and share solutions to interoperability problems in their domain. The conference included participants from a variety of perspectives

including manufacturing, eBusiness, standards development, and bioscience. Conference session topics included manufacturing systems integration, long-term data retention, advanced semantic language development, digital image search, sensor integration, and enterprise integration. During the Interoperability Week, NIST's technical staff actively contributed to workshops such as "Exploring Identity Management: Global Landscape and Implications for Stakeholder Engagement Around the National Response Framework," and the Ontology Summit 2008.

National Archives Records Administration Governance Issues

MEL was invited to contribute to a National Archives and Records Administration workshop held on November 14-15, 2007 to discuss governance issues for the Global Digital Format Registry (GDFR), a distributed system to store, discover, and deliver representation information about digital formats. An MIP Staff representative spoke about the archival of engineering information and advocated that the GDFR should make it easy for user communities representing a particular domain to tailor the GDFR data model and classification scheme to their needs. He also gave an overview of the themes that emerged from the 2006 and 2007 NIST Interoperability Week workshops and discussed NIST's proposal to extend the Open Archival Information System reference model by taking different access scenarios into account.

Symposium on Medical Device Supply Chains

NIST co-sponsored a symposium entitled "Medical Device Supply Chain Management and Standards" held in Minneapolis, Minnesota, on November 16, 2007. About 100 participants representing major medical device OEM and first-tier suppliers, health care providers, state and federal governments, and academia attended the symposium. Necessary information and communication standards were identified as a critical component in the medical device industry for supporting supply chain optimization, tracing and tracking expensive medical devices, and ensuring product quality and safety. For more information: http://www.ie.umn.edu/cscr/symposium/index.htm.

French/United States Manufacturing-Related IT Workshop

NIST Associates, along with the French Embassy organized and hosted a two-day French-U.S. Workshop on "Information and Communications Technology (ICT) and Standards for Supply Chains and Product Lifecycle Management (PLM)," held at NIST November 6-7, 2007. There were about 40 invited participants from the United States and France representing universities, laboratories, the European Commission, NIST, and funding agencies from both countries. Dr. Hratch G. Semerjian, NIST Chief Scientist, opened the Workshop with an emphasis on the importance of global trade, information technology, and international cooperation. His talk was followed by a talk by Dr. Simon Szykman, Director of the National Coordination Office for Networking and IT R&D (NITRD). On the second day, Maj. Gen. John Phillips (retired, but who was Deputy Assistant Secretary for the Department of Defense (DoD)/Logistics) gave a talk from the perspective of the military services. MG Phillips pointed out that the cost of supply chain and logistics for DoD is $170B/yr. He stressed that the use of ICT is critical to achieve cost-effectiveness of defense systems. Dr. Prabir Bagchi, Professor of Operations and Supply Chain Management at George Washington University Business School, gave a talk from a business enterprise perspective on the importance of supply chain management, reverse logistics, and product design for global competitiveness. There was general consensus that the research program as envisioned would require a collaborative approach that leverages the socio-cultural practices, experiences, and competencies of Europe and the United States in creating valid and useful methods and support systems. Sanjay Jain and André Craens participated in the U.S.-French Workshop held at NIST and presented their work on "Virtual Environment for Supply Chain Interoperability Standards Evaluation." Participants presented their research efforts and discussed potential collaborative project themes. A report on the workshop detailing the proceedings is under preparation and will be made available on completion at this website: http://iutcerral.univ-lyon2.fr/fr_us_workshop_06/.

Interoperability Week, 2007

NIST hosted its second annual Interoperability Week in Gaithersburg, Maryland, April 23-25, 2007. The Interoperability Week Conference provided a venue for people from different disciplines to network, compare issues, and share solutions to interoperability problems in their domain. The conference included participants from a variety of perspectives including manufacturing, communications, supply chain, and science. Conference session topics included manufacturing systems integration, long-term data retention with an emphasis on product engineering media, advanced semantic language development, digital 2D and 3D image research, and federal enterprise integration. The plenary session featured speakers from Microsoft, the World Wide Web Consortium, and U.S. National Archives.

Open Applications Group Meeting

NIST hosted the Open Applications Group, Inc. (OAGi) meeting May 2-5, 2006. The OAGi is a not-for-profit open standards group building process-based XML standards for both B2B and application-to-application integration. NIST and OAGi have collaborated on several projects to develop validation and testing resources for the manufacturing and business standards communities. Presentations given at the meeting can be found at: http://www.openapplications.org/downloads/meetings/20060502-Gaithersburg/20060502-Gaithersburg-Agenda.htm.

Interoperability Week, 2006

NIST's MIP sponsored and hosted the first Interoperability Week at NIST during March 2006. Over 250 participants took part in nine separate meetings during the week. The highlight of the week was the plenary session with remarks by NIST Director Bill Jeffrey and presentations by: Olwen Huxley, Staff member, U.S. House of Representatives, Committee on Science, Subcommittee on Environment, Technology and Standards; Karla Norsworthy, Vice President of Software Standards for IBM Corporation; and Jim Turner, Chief Minority Counsel, U.S. House of Representatives, Committee on Science.

The concept of Interoperability Week arose from within MSID as many staff members contribute technically to a plethora of standards development working groups, committees, and consortia with a key interest in resolving interoperability issues across the enterprise and supply chain. NIST wanted to provide an opportunity to gather some of these worldwide forces for interoperability so that they could continue their work, assist the community to learn of each other, and perhaps provide some informal opportunities to network across organizations. Additional information can be found at http://www.mel.nist.gov/div826/msid/sima/interopweek/meetings.htm, and some articles in the public press can be viewed at http://www.mel.nist.gov/msid/msidnews.htm.

Semantic Web Enabled Software Engineering Workshop

MEL ran a successful workshop on Semantic Web Enabled Software Engineering (SWESE) at the International Semantic Web Conference held in Galway, in Ireland November 2006. Over the past five years there have been attempts to bring together languages and tools developed for Software Engineering with Semantic Web languages. One of the most recent of these attempts is the development of OMG's ODM. Until recently, this work has been motivated largely by an interest to exploit the popularity and features of UML tools for the creation of vocabularies and ontologies for the Semantic Web. What are the potential benefits related to the reversal of this approach and the use of Semantic Web concepts in the field of Software Engineering? A packed room heard fourteen presentations, including two by NIST staff, on how semantic web technologies could improve software development. Participants were encouraged by the potential of this and developed plans to create a virtual community to continue to pursue this vision.

First Indo-U.S. Workshop on Engineering Design

NIST provided the U.S. Chair of the First Indo-U.S. workshop on Design Engineering, January 5-7, 2006, in Bangalore, India. The Indo-U.S. Workshop was organized jointly by the Indian Institute of Science, Bangalore, and Carnegie Melon University, at Hotel Chancery, Bangalore. This workshop was funded by the Indo-U.S. Science and Technology Forum. The eventual goal of the workshop is to create a forum for research interaction between researchers in India and the United States. There were about 70 participants from India and 17 from the United States for this first event. U.S. delegates represented diverse domains, including sociology, engineering, public policy, industry, and the government.

International Federation for Information Processing (IFIP) International Conference

NIST and Enterprise Integration Inc. (EII) co-sponsored an IFIP conference in September 2005 on how computer programs for business models, modeling and simulation methodologies, and automation tools and technology can be used in concert to offer manufacturing enterprises a competitive advantage. IFIP is an umbrella organization for national societies working in the field of information technology. It is a non-governmental, non-profit organization with offices in Austria. Its members include over 48 national societies and academies of science.

Long-Term Knowledge Retention Workshops

MEL organized and hosted a series of meetings from August 2005 through April 2007 bringing together experts from government, industry, and universities to improve coordination of research efforts in representing and managing archives of engineering design data. Major stakeholders from the National Archives and Library of Congress participated as well. These meetings led to current collaborations with Naval Surface Warfare Center – Carderock Division and the UK Office of Library Networking to solve engineering information long-term retention problems, and also to the ideas successfully presented in the paper "Sustaining Engineering Informatics: Toward Methods and Metrics for Digital Curation" at the 3rd International Digital Curation Conference in Washington DC, December 12-13, 2007.

6. The Spawning of Other Programs

In its three years of existence, MIP has focused its activities, working with industry to develop and test standards and testing infrastructures. Now the Manufacturing Systems Integration Division is ready to:
- Expand upon its national or international standards development and testing presence including
  - Testing methods, metrics & conformance criteria
  - Automated testing tools
- Expand its involvement in industry-led manufacturing integration pilot projects
- Further its investment in semantic standards and technology research

But even with all of the many successes of the Manufacturing Interoperability Program, system interoperability and the manufacturing lifecycle still face challenges yet to be resolved. As MIP came to a close, there were ideals remaining that would build upon MIP's legacy:

- To prepare for a future where products are 100% recyclable, where complete disassembly of a product at its end of life is routine. Where manufacturing itself has a zero-net impact on the environment. We need to develop a set of validated information models for lifecycle information-based manufacturing and sustainability that support interoperability among tools and standards for design, analysis, lifecycle assessment, and information management.

- To establish a facility for dynamic model-based interoperability testing of manufacturing software applications. Manufacturing systems developed by different software vendors are typically incapable of working together. The costs and delays associated with developing custom integrations of manufacturing software hurt U.S. productivity and competitiveness. Software applications continue to evolve and interoperability is expected to remain a problem. Although NIST has developed static testing tools that, for example, check data formats, these tools can only go so far. Ultimately, software applications must be tested against live operational systems. It is impractical to use real industrial systems to support dynamic interoperability testing and research due to:
  - Access issues - manufacturing facilities are not open to outsiders, as proprietary data and processes may be compromised.
  - Technical issues - operational systems are not instrumented to support testing.
  - Cost issues - productivity suffers when actual production systems are taken offline to support testing.

No facility with open interfaces currently exists to support dynamic interoperability testing for a broad range of manufacturing interface standards and software applications. Prohibitive development costs and other priorities prevent most software vendors, research, and standards organizations from developing systems to support interoperability testing.

- To reduce the high cost of exchanging information across the entire, global supply chain. These costs are incurred, to varying degrees, by all participants. Recently implemented outsourcing and off-shoring policies have resulted in major changes to the number, the nature, and the location of those participants. More and more, OEMs are becoming system assemblers and their products are conceived, designed, engineered, fabricated, transported, stored, and sold by participants in different parts of the world, including being dispersed across the United States. These changes have fueled dramatic increases in the (1) movement of materials, components, and sub-systems, (2) the collaboration in design, engineering, and planning among those participants, and (3) awareness of the supply chain supporting these exchanges, and the fragility of its effectiveness. The payback on improved supply chain management is already known: a $1 reduction in cost from supply chain efficiencies is equivalent to a $12 increase in sales revenues[69]. These increases have been accompanied by an explosion in the amount of information exchange and the complexity of information being exchanged. The ability of U.S. manufacturers to compete in a global marketplace is dependent on access to a low cost, widely accepted, open, and efficient information exchange infrastructure.

Bearing in mind these continuing goals, further standardization and metrology for manufacturing will be developed within the context of two new programs: Sustainable and Lifecycle Information-based Manufacturing and Supply Chain Integration.

Sustainable and Lifecycle Information-based Manufacturing (SLIM) Program

Program Strategy:

Sustainable manufacturing systems require a systemic view that encompasses product lifecycle management, process models, infrastructure technologies, and semantically interoperable information exchange over extended networked enterprises. The full product life cycle involves many complex processes and employs numerous computer-based applications and systems. Realizing such a system depends on: 1) semantically accurate modeling, capturing, manipulating, exchanging, and using of information in all product life cycle decision-making processes, across all application domains, and 2) a trusted system of measures to support the nation's ability to monitor energy consumption, hazardous materials usage, and carbon output throughout the life of manufactured goods, from raw material extraction, through production, throughout the use of a product, and including the ultimate disposal, recycling, remanufacturing or reclamation of the components.

The program has three major objectives:

Objective 1: Establish standards requirements for sustainable manufacturing

The following tasks will be undertaken to achieve this objective:
- Survey existing documentary standards and performance metrics landscape for sustainable manufacturing. Perform case studies of existing implementations of sustainable manufacturing to generate information requirements for sustainability and characterize economic, ecological, and societal interactions in a product's lifecycle. Propose new or harmonized standards and metrics for sustainable manufacturing.
- Characterize business in support of long-term access to lifecycle information to a unified accounting scheme for support of sustainable design, manufacturing, use, and disposal of products. Develop green accounting principles to trace the environmental impacts from the part level to the system level and for the full lifecycle, including assembly, disassembly, and recycling.
- Characterize engineering information in support of long-term access to lifecycle information. Develop and test a framework for engineering information archives.

---

[69] Florida International University, College of Business Administration, Ryder Center for Supply Chain Management, http://business.fiu.edu/centers/ryder.cfm [as of 02/11/2008].

Objective 2: Provide formal models of product and process information

The following tasks will be undertaken to achieve this objective:
- Develop information models for products and manufacturing processes that provide key attributes that are necessary for sustainable and lifecycle information-based manufacturing. Present the resulting integrated formal information model(s) to industry consortia and standards development organizations.
- Develop and validate high-priority standards for seamless information exchange between engineering and production, and between production and manufacturing business functions. Enable reuse of existing manufacturing data standards within an evolving standards infrastructure, and help manufacturers ensure that established and widely-implemented engineering and product data standards can be retooled.

Objective 3: Develop validation and testing methodologies for information models

The following tasks will be undertaken to achieve this objective:
- Develop model-based validation and testing techniques for sustainable and lifecycle information-based manufacturing.
- Create test scenarios for validation of information model standards for interoperability of tools and systems. Develop a testbed that validates the different aspects of the work conducted throughout this project. The testbed will apply metrics for the performance of specific applications or procedures for sustainable and lifecycle information-based manufacturing.

Supply Chain Integration Program

Program Strategy:

The goal of this program is a testing and standards infrastructure that enables the automated exchange of critical information across the entire supply chain. The program will focus on information exchanges between logistics providers and between designers and fabricators. Two major projects, which were initiated under MIP, will be concluded. They include the development of models, methods, and tools to enable conformance testing of individual logistics applications against existing standards and interoperability testing of multiple logistics applications using those standards. The third near-term project seeks to address requirements the manufacturing sector has set forward for critical infrastructure standards including UML and OWL.

In FY08, we initiated one major project that focuses on an important problem: how designers automatically find fabricators who can satisfy design requirements. Unlike logistics and IV&I, a complete set of business-process and information-exchange standards do not exist at this time. We plan to use PSL for the business process and a combination of UML and OWL for the information exchanges.

The Program has three major objectives.

Objective 1: Propose new supply-chain standards

Today's supply-chain integration standards are inadequate. They are large, monolithic, complicated specifications that capture only the format and syntax of information, and do not capture the real meaning of the manufacturing information they are meant to convey. They are usually developed without any thought given (1) to validating against the original manufacturing requirements or (2) to testing against commercial software applications. Additionally, they are not expressed in a computer-interpretable language that supports automated exchange.

To address these shortcomings, we will work with Standard Development Organizations to develop a new workflow process that will result in standards that can be validated and tested more easily. We will work with industry to develop rules that allow large interface specifications to be decomposed into atomic elements that can be tested individually and then reassembled automatically. We will use recently developed formal languages, which can represent meaning in ways that computers can understand and analyze, to build these atomic elements.

Objective 2: Expand existing testing processes

Before partners buy supply-chain software applications, they will want assurances that these applications implement new interface standards correctly. The current conformance and interoperability testing tools, which require a significant amount of human involvement, will not work for these new types of standards because they test for syntax and formats only. Developing new testing methods that specifically address information content will require an entirely new approach.

To develop these new tools, we will collaborate with our university partners and researchers from NIST's Information Technology Laboratory to develop a distance metric that provides a quantitative basis for comparing the representations of two manufacturing information terms. This metric should have two main properties: it should be zero when two terms are identical in meaning and it should increase as the differences between the meanings of the two terms increase. Using this new metric, we will collaborate with our industry partners to develop new, automated tools to test conformance against selected interface standards. The output from these tools will provide the information needed for integrating the commercial software applications typically used in specific supply-chain scenarios.

Objective 3: Develop new integration techniques

Today, almost all of the information exchanged between supply-chain partners takes place after a business arrangement has been established. Based on our virtual-supplier-network vision and the anticipated explosion of new software services on the Web, this situation is expected to change dramatically. Using these services, small business will be able to advertise its capabilities and OEMs will be able to post their product requirements on the Web. Some of these services will seek to match capabilities to requirements thereby initiating a new business arrangement. Other services will provide a monitoring capability to track the entire business process from design to production to delivery and manage the associated information exchanges.

New techniques and knowledge representations will be needed to integrate these services and to realize this novel business collaboration model. We will propose standard representations for describing, and standard methods for accessing supplier capabilities and OEM requirements. We will collaborate with industry to (1) develop prototype business registries and repositories to house those descriptions, (2) provide methods and tools for discovering partners based on these descriptions, and (3) propose techniques for integrating these new Web-based services. These methods, tools, and techniques - together with the atomic standards described above - will allow companies to dynamically form, collaborate, and dissolve based on changing market conditions and customer demands.

7. Conclusion

Over the course of the Manufacturing Interoperability Program, great strides were made in advancing standards, developing testing methods and software, and integrating systems. Our work in standards encompassed gap analysis, drafting of specifications, leading the technical development of standards side-by-side with industry, and facilitating environments to harmonize existing and sometimes conflicting standards responding to the same functional requirements. We helped advance the adoption and commercialization of standardized solutions by building testing environments that provided persistent validation of developing standards, conformance testing of implementations adopting standards, and interoperability testing using real-time data sets among industry partners in the supply chain. Both standardization and testing activities contributed to furthering the integration of manufacturing systems within a corporate enterprise and across its supporting supply chain.

As technology and market globalization evolves at an ever more rapid pace, our work in building manufacturing interoperability solutions is not yet done. But our investment over these last several years toward this goal has provided palpable results for the manufacturing community and our industrial partners.

8. Acknowledgements

My thanks and appreciation go to all the division leadership and MIP-funded staff for their contribution to this publication. Most of the content drew upon existing internal white papers, presentations, and program or project write-ups to produce this final summary on the Manufacturing Interoperability Program.

9. Disclaimer

Mention of commercial products or services in this paper does not imply approval or endorsement by NIST, nor does it imply that such products or services are necessarily the best available for the purpose.

Publications

The following is a list of the publications related to the Manufacturing Interoperability Program. If you would like to identify those papers published on a particular topic, or by a particular author, please see our MSID Publications available on the web: http://www.mel.nist.gov/msidlibrary/publications.html

J. Lubell, B. Harvey, P. Goyal, K. Morris, *"NDR Profile Schema Version 1.0 User Guide"* NIST Interagency/Internal Report (NISTIR 7547) (PubID: 824742)

C. Bock, *"Part-part Relations in an RDF/S and OWL Extension"* NIST Interagency/Internal Report (NISTIR 7507) (PubID: 824673)

X. Zha, R. Sriram, M. Fernandez, F. Mistree, *"Knowledge-Intensive Collaborative Decision Support for Design Processes: A Hybrid? Decision Support Model and Agent"* Computers in Industry (PubID: 824714)

Y.T. T. Lee, F. Riddick, C. McLean, S. K. Leong, *"Current Activities Related to the Core Manufacturing Simulation Data Standards Development Effort"* Proceedings of the Fall 2008 Simulation Interoperability Workshop, Orlando, FL, United States (PubID: 824688)

G. Ameta, R. Sudarsan, X. Fiorentini, M. Mani, S. Fenves, K. Lyons, R. Sriram, *"Extending the Notion of Quality from Physical Metrology to Information and Sustainability"* NIST Interagency/Internal Report (NISTIR 7517) (PubID: 824666)

F. Riddick, Y.T. T. Lee, *"Representing Layout Information In The Cmsd Specification"* 2008 Winter Simulation Conference, Miami, FL, United States (PubID: 824678)

S. K. Leong, M. Johansson, B. Johansson, Y.T. T. Lee, F. Riddick, *"A Real World Pilot implementation of the Core Manufacturing Simulation Information Model"* Proceedings of the Simulation Interoperability Standards Organization (SISO) Spring 2008 SIW Workshop, 2008 Euro Simulation Interoperability Workshop, Edinburgh, Scotland, United States (PubID: 824670)

D. Kibira, C. McLean, *"Modeling and Simulation for Sustainable Manufacturing"* Proceedings of the 2nd IASTED 2008 Africa Conference on Modeling and Simulation, Science And Technology Innovation For Sustainable Development, Gaborone, Botswana (PubID: 824675)

V. Liang, C. Bock, X. Zha, *"An Ontological Modeling Platform"* NIST Interagency/Internal Report (NISTIR 7509) (PubID: 824674)

P. Hoffmann, S. Feng, G. Ameta, P. Ghodous, L. Qiao, *"Towards a Multi-View Semantic Model for Product Feature Description"* Concurrent Engineering 2008, Belfast, 07/24/2008 to 07/25/2008 (PubID: 824657)

P. Denno, T. Thurman, J. Mettenburg, D. Hardy, *"On Enabling a Model-based Systems Engineering Discipline"* The 18th International Symposium of the International Council on Systems Engineering (INCOSE), The Netherlands, Netherlands (PubID: 824653)

J. Lubell, R. Sudarsan, E. Subrahmanian, M. Mani, *"Sustaining Engineering Informatics: Toward Methods and Metrics for Digital Curation"* International Journal of Digital Curation (PubID: 824667)

K. Morris, P. Goyal, S. P. Frechette, *"Development Life Cycle and Tools for Data Exchange Specification"* Proceedings of the ASME 2008 International Design Engineering Technical Conferences & Computers and Information in Engineering Conference, IDETC/CIE 2008, Brooklyn, NY, United States (PubID: 824658)

C. P. Cheng, J. Pan, G. Lau, K. Law, A. Jones, *"Relating Taxonomies with Regulations"* Proceedings of the 9th Annual International Conference on Digital Government Research, Montreal, Canada (PubID: 824637)

M. Mani, K. Lyons, R. Sudarsan, E. Subrahmanian, R. Sriram, *"Introducing Sustainability Early into Manufacturing Process Planning"* Proceedings of the 14th International Conference on Manufacturing Science and Engineering, ASME, Evanston, IL (PubID: 824645)

X. Fiorentini, R. Sudarsan, M. Mani, S. Fenves, R. Sriram, *"An Evaluation of Description Logic for the Development of Product Models"* NIST Interagency/Internal Report (NISTIR 7481) (PubID: 824437)

J. Kim, B. Kulvatunyou, N. Ivezic, A. Jones, *"A Layered Approach to Semantic Similarity Analysis of XML Schemas"* Proceedings of the 2008 IEEE International Conference on Information Reuse and Integration, Las Vegas, NV (PubID: 824640)

J. Lubell, M. Mani, E. Subrahmanian, R. Sudarsan, *"Long Term Sustainment Workshop Report"* NIST Interagency/Internal Report (NISTIR 7496) (PubID: 824648)

R. Sudarsan, E. Subrahmanian, *"Engineering Informatics: Introduction to the Special Issue"* Journal of Computing and Information Science in Engineering (PubID: 823046)

R. Sriram, A. Deshmukh, A. Banerjee, S. Gupta, *"Content-Based Assembly Search: A Step Towards Assembly Reuse"* Journal of CAD (PubID: 824442)

M. Vujasinovic, N. Ivezic, B. Kulvatunyou, E. Barkmeyer, M. Missikoff, F. Taglino, Z. Marjanovic, I. Miletic, *"An Industrial Validation of a Semantic Mediation Architecture"* IEEE Internet Computing (PubID: 823014)

B. Kulvatunyou, K. Morris, S. P. Frechette, *"Development Life Cycle for Semantically Coherent Data Exchange Specification "* Concurrent Engineering-Research and Applications (PubID: 824671)

D. Libes, T. O'Connell, *"Applying Serious Games to Intelligence Analysis"* Proceedings of the 11th IASTED International Conference on Software Engineering and Apps (SEA 2007), Cambridge, MA (PubID: 822743)

S. Rachuri, R. Sriram, M. Sarigecili, M. Baysal, U. Roy, *"An Evaluation Mechanism for Defining Gaps and Overlaps of Product Information Exchange Standards"* Proceedings of the IMECE '2007 Conference, Seattle, WA (PubID: 822747)

J. Lubell, S. Rachuri, E. Subrahmanian, M. Mani, *"Sustaining Engineering Informatics: Toward Methods and Metrics for Digital Curation"* Proceedings of the 3rd International Digital Curation Conference, Washington, DC (PubID: 822746)

S. Rachuri, *"Science based Information Metrology for Engineering Informatics "* PerMIS '07, Gaithersburg, MD (PubID: 822745)

J. Kim, M. Pratt, R. Iyer, R. Sriram, *"Standardized Data Exchange of CAD Models with Design Intent"* Journal of CAD

(PubID: 822750)

C. Bock, X. Zha, *"Ontological Product Modeling for Collaborative Design"* Advanced Engineering Informatics (PubID: 822748)

C. McLean, *"Distributed Simulation - A Necessity or Ivory Tower Research?"* Proceedings of the Winter Simulation Conference 2007, Washington, DC (PubID: 822739)

X. Fiorentini, I. Gambino, V. Liang, S. Foufou, S. Rachuri, M. Mani, C. Bock, *"An Ontology for Assembly Representation"* NIST Interagency/Internal Report (NISTIR 7436) (PubID: 822740)

N. Ivezic, B. Kulvatunyou, M. Vujasinovic, P. Snack, Z. Marjanovic, H. Cho, *"Standards-Based Semantic Middleware"* Proceedings of the eChallenges 2007 Conference and Exhibition, The Hague, Netherlands (PubID: 822738)

S. Jain, C. McLean, Y.T. T. Lee, *"Towards Standards for Integrated Gaming and Simulation for Incident Management"* Proceedings of the 2007 Summer Computer Simulation Conference (PubID: 822330)

Y.T. T. Lee, S. K. Leong, F. Riddick, M. Johansson, B. J. Johansson, *"A Pilot Implementation of the Core Manufacturing Simulation Data Information Model"* Proceedings of the Systems Interoperability Standards Organization 2007 Fall Simulation Interoperability Workshop (PubID: 822736)

D. Kibira, C. McLean, *"Generic Simulation of Automotive Assembly for Interoperability Testing"* Proceedings of the 2007 Winter Simulation Conference (PubID: 822737)

M. Johansson, S. K. Leong, Y.T. T. Lee, F. Riddick, G. Shao, B. J. Johansson, A. Skoogh, P. Klingstam, *"A Test Implementation of the Core Manufacturing Simulation Data Specification"* Proceedings of the 2007 Winter Simulation Conference (PubID: 822734)

E. Subrahmanian, Y. Reich, *"Advancing Problem Definition and Concept Generation for Improved Product Life Cycle Management"* NIST Interagency/Internal Report (NISTIR 7430) (PubID: 822328)

S. Jain, F. Riddick, A. Craens, D. Kibira, *"Distributed Simulation for Interoperability Testing Along the Supply Chain"* Proceedings of the 2007 Winter Simulation Conference (PubID: 822735)

J. Kim, M. Pratt, R. Iyer, R. Sriram, *"Data Exchange of Parametric CAD Models Using ISO 10303-108"* NIST Interagency/Internal Report (NISTIR 7433) (PubID: 822720)

B. Jeong, J. Woo, H. Cho, B. Kulvatunyou, J. Lee, *"A Web Service-Based Reconfigurable Testbed for Business-to-Business (B2B) Integration"* Proceedings of the IEEE International Conference on Web Services, International Conference on Web Services (ICWS) (PubID: 822715)

C. McLean, S. Jain, A. Craens, D. Kibira, *"A Virtual Manufacturing Environment for Interoperability Testing"* Proceedings of the Delft University of Technology Conference, Netherlands (PubID: 822713)

C. McLean, S. Jain, F. Riddick, Y.T. T. Lee, *"A Simulation Architecture for Manufacturing Interoperability Testing"* Proceedings of the Summer Computer Simulation Conference '07, San Diego, CA (PubID: 822712)

B. Kulvatunyou, J. Jang, B. Jeong, J. Chang, H. Cho, *"Discovering and Integrating Distributed Manufacturing Services with Semantic Manufacturing Capability Profile"* International Journal of Computer Integrated Manufacturing (PubID: 822705)

B. Kulvatunyou, B. Jeong, D. Lee, H. Cho, *"A Novel Approach to Measuring Structural Similarity Between XML Documents"* Proceedings of the 20th International Conference on Industrial Engineering and Other Applications of Applied Intelligent Systems (PubID: 822706)

S. Jayaram, U. Jayaram, Y. Kim, C. Dechenne, K. Lyons, C. Palmer, T. Mitsui, *"Industry Case Studies in the Use of Immersive Virtual Assembly"* Virtual Reality Journal (PubID: 822709)

E. Barkmeyer, B. Kulvatunyou, *"An Ontology for the e-Kanban Business Process"* NIST Interagency/Internal Report (NISTIR 7404) (PubID: 822708)

I. Novicic, Z. Kokovic, N. Jakovljevic, V. Ljubicic, M. Bacetic, N. Anicic, Z. Marjanovic, N. Ivezic, *"A Case Study in Business Applications Development Using Open Source and Semantic Web Technologies"* Proceedings of the 3rd International Conference on Interoperability for Enterprise Software and Applications (IESA "07), Conference on Interoperability for Enterprise Software and Applications, Funchal, Madeira Island (PubID: 822659)

B. Kulvatunyou, N. Ivezic, A. Jones, Y. Peng, Z. Ding, R. Pan, Y. Yu, H. Cho, *"A Probabilistic Framework for Semantic Similarity and Ontology Mapping"* Proceedings of the 2007 Industrial Engineering Research Conference (PubID: 822710)

E. Barkmeyer, P. Denno, *"On Capturing Information Requirements in Process Specifications"* Proceedings of the 3rd International Conference on Interoperability for Enterprise Software and Applications (IESA "07) (PubID: 822655)

Y. Luo, Y.T. T. Lee, *"Data Exchange Strategy for Manufacturing Simulation of Shop Floor Information Systems"* International Journal of Manufacturing Technology and Management (IJMTM) (PubID: 822654)

M. Jankovic, N. Ivezic, T. Knothe, Z. Marjanovic, P. Snack, *"A Case Study in Enterprise Modelling for Interoperable Cross-Enterprise Data Exchange"* Proceedings of the 3rd International Conference on Interoperability for Enterprise Software and Applications (IESA '07) (PubID: 822657)

I. Miletic, M. Vujasinovic, N. Ivezic, Z. Marjanovic, *"Enabling Semantic Mediation for Business Applications: XML-RDF, RDF-XML and XSD-RDFS Transformations"* Proceedings of the 3rd International Conference on Interoperability for Enterprise Software and Applications (IESA "07) (PubID: 822656)

B. Kulvatunyou, J. Kim, *"An Interactive Procedure for Efficient Testing of B2B: A Case in Messaging Service Tests"* 3rd International Conference on Interoperability for Enterprise Software Applications (PubID: 822650)

N. Ivezic, P. Snack, *"An Athena Validation Pilot Showcase for Automotive Industry"* AIAG ATHENA Project Newsletter (PubID: 822649)

P. Denno, *"MOSS - Material Off-Shore Sourcing"* Automotive Industry Action Group (AIAG) ActionLine Magazine (PubID: 822648)

B. Kulvatunyou, J. Durand, J. Woo, M. Martin, *"Testing and Monitoring E-Business Using the Event-Driven Test Scripting Language"* 3rd International Conference on Interoperability for Enterprise Software (PubID: 822652)

Y.T. T. Lee, Y. Luo, *"Machine Shop Information Model Application, Next Step"* NIST Interagency/Internal Report (NISTIR 7388) (PubID: 822651)

J. Lubell, S. Rachuri, E. Subrahmanian, W. Regli, *"Long Term Knowledge Retention Workshop Summary"* NIST Interagency/Internal Report (NISTIR 7386) (PubID: 822647)

Y. Luo, Y.T. T. Lee, *"The Interface Development for Machine Shop Simulation"* International Journal of Knowledge Management Studies, Vol. 1:3/4 (PubID: 822637)

S. Brockmans, R. Colomb, P. Haase, E. Kendall, E. Wallace, G. Xie, *"A Model-Driven Approach for Building OWL DL and OWL Full Ontologies"* Proceedings of the International Semantic Web Conference (ISWC) (PubID: 822636)

E. L. Morse, M. P. Steves, J. Scholtz, *"Metrics and Methodologies for Evaluating Technologies for Intelligence Analysts"* Proceedings of the 2005 International Conference on Intelligence Analysis (PubID: 822638)

C. Bock, *"Interprocess Communication in the Process Specification Language"* NIST Interagency/Internal Report (NISTIR 7348) (PubID: 822634)

P. Denno, *"Notes on an Information Model for Production Rules"* NIST Interagency/Internal Report (NISTIR 7363) (PubID: 822641)

D. Libes, E. L. Morse, J. Scholtz, *"A Study on Search Engine Use by Intelligence Analysts"* 18th IASTED International Conference on Parallel and Distributed Computing Systems, Dallas, TX (PubID: 822628)

P. Denno, N. Ivezic, *"Message Validation with a Semantic Reasoning Tools"* NIST Interagency/Internal Report (NISTIR 7347) (PubID: 822629)

C. Bock, *"Part-part Relations in an RDF/S and OWL Extension"* Journal of Web Semantics (PubID: 822630)

L. Obrst, B. Ashpole, W. Ceusters, M. Mani, S. R. Ray, B. Smith, *"The Evaluation of Ontologies"* Semantic Web: Revolutionizing Knowledge Discovery in the Life Sciences, Springer (PubID: 822618)

B. Kulvatunyou, B. Jeong, H. Cho, N. Ivezic, A. Jones, *"Evaluating Suitability for Replacement of an Integrated Software Component"* Proceedings of the Schema Matchmaking and Resource Retrieval Workshop, VLDB Conference, to , (01-Aug-2006) (PubID: 822622)

J. Woo, H. Cho, B. Kulvatunyou, *"Allocation of Manufacturers through Internet-based Collaboration for Distributed Process Planning"* International Journal of Production Research (PubID: 822617)

S. K. Leong, Y.T. T. Lee, F. Riddick, *"A Core Manufacturing Simulation Data Information Model for Manufacturing Applications"* Proceedings of the Systems Interoperability Standards Organization 2006 Fall Simulation Interoperability Workshop (PubID: 822625)

X. Zha, R. Sriram, *"Platform-based Product Design and Development: A Knowledge Intensive Support Approach"* Journal of Knowledge-based Systems (PubID: 822620)

X. Zha, R. Sriram, *"Feature Technology and Ontology for Embedded System Design and Development"* Proceedings of the DETC 2006 ASME Design Engineering Technical Conference, Philadelphia, PA (PubID: 822626)

N. Ivezic, E. Barkmeyer, B. Kulvatunyou, A. Jones, P. Snack, Z. Marjanovic, H. Cho, *"A Validation Architecture for Advanced Interoperability Provisioning"* Proceedings of the 2006 e-Challenges Conference (PubID: 822619)

M.S. Li, A. Deshmukh, A. Jones, *"An Infrastructure to Support Performance Analysis in Complex Systems"* Proceedings of the PERMIS Conference, PerMIS, Gaithersburg, MD (PubID: 822623)

S. Rachuri, S. Foufou, S. Kemmerer, *"Analysis of Standards for Lifecycle Management of Systems for US Army --- a preliminary investigation"* NIST Interagency/Internal Report (NISTIR 7339 (PubID: 822627)

G. Shao, C. McLean, S. K. Leong, *"User Interface of Simulation of the Shipbuilding Operations"* NIST Interagency/Internal Report (NISTIR 7320) (PubID: 822610)

R. Sriram, S. Szykman, D. Durham, *"Special Issue on Collaborative Engineering"* To appear in the Journal of Computing and Information Science in Engineering (JCISE) (PubID: 822614)

A. Biswas, S. Fenves, V. Shapiro, R. Sriram, *"Representation of Heterogeneous Material Properties in the Core Product Model"* To appear in Engineering with Computers (PubID: 822612)

J. Lubell, B. Kulvatunyou, K. Morris, B. Harvey, *"Implementing XML Schema Naming and Design Rules"* Proceedings of the Extreme Markup Languages 2006 Conference (PubID: 822609)

L. Obrst, P. Cassidy, S. R. Ray, B. Smith, D. Soergel, M. West, P. Yim, *"The 2006 Upper Ontology Summit Joint Communique"* To appear in the Applied Ontology Journal (PubID: 822611)

C. Bock, M. Gruninger, D. Libes, J. Lubell, E. Subrahmanian, *"Evaluating Reasoning Systems"* NIST Interagency/Internal Report (NISTIR 7310) (PubID: 822613)

S. R. Ray, A. Jones, *"Manufacturing Interoperability"* Special Issue of JIM - Journal of Intelligent Manufacturing (International Scientific Journal), Vol. 17, No. 6, pp. 681-688 (PubID: 822140)

L. Obrst, L. Hughes, S. R. Ray, *"Prospects and Possibilities for Ontology Evaluation: The View from NCOR"* Proceedings of the 4th International EON Workshop - Evaluation of Ontologies for the Web (PubID: 822500)

N. Anicic, Z. Marjanovic, N. Ivezic, A. Jones, *"Semantic Enterprise Application Integration Standards"* International Journal of Manufacturing Technology and Management (IJMTM) (PubID: 822499)

S. Rachuri, Y. Han, S. Foufou, S. Feng, U. Roy, F. Wang, R. Sriram, K. Lyons, *"Assembly Model Representation from Conceptual to the Detailed Design"* Journal of Computing and Information Science in Engineering (PubID: 822267)

Y.T. T. Lee, C. McLean, Y. Luo, *"Information Modeling and Model Implementation"* Proceedings of the International Simulation Conference 2006, Palermo, Italy (PubID: 822353)

L. Deshayes, S. Foufou, M. Gruninger, *"An Ontology Architecture for Standards Integration and Conformance in*

Manufacturing" Proceedings of the IDMME 2006, Grenoble, France (PubID: 822357)

R. Sriram, *"Artificial Intelligence in Engineering: Personal Reflections"* Editorial to appear in Advanced Engineering Informatics (PubID: 822351)

S. Feng, *"Preliminary Design and Manufacturing Planning Integration Using Web-Based Intelligent Agents"* Journal of Intelligent Manufacturing, Vol. 16:4-5, pp. 423-437 (PubID: 822352)

A. Deshmukh, M. Karnik, S. Gupta, R. Sriram, *"A System for Performing Content-Based Searches on a Database of Mechanical Assemblies"* Proceedings of IMECE2005, 2005 ASME International Mechanical Engineering Congress and Exposition, Orlando, FL (PubID: 822355)

E. Subrahmanian, S. Rachuri, A. Bouras, S. Fenves, S. Foufou, R. Sriram, *"The Role of Standards in Product Lifecycle Management Support"* NIST Interagency/Internal Report (NISTIR 7289) (PubID: 822354)

X. Zha, S. Fenves, R. Sriram, *"A Feature-Based Approach to Embedded System Hardware and Software Co-Design"* Proceedings of the DETC 2005 ASME Design Engineering Technical Conference, Long Beach, CA (PubID: 822335)

S. Kemmerer, *"NIST Supply Chain Integration Solutions"* Manufacturing Interoperability Program Supply Chain Brochure (PubID: 822325)

L. Patil, R. Sriram, *"Ontology Formalization of Product Semantics for Product Lifecycle Management"* NIST Interagency/Internal Report (NISTIR 7274) (PubID: 822326)

X. Zha, R. Sriram, *"Knowledge-Intensive Collaborative Decision Support for Design Process"* Intelligent Decision-Making Support Systems (i-DMSS): Foundations, Applications and Challenges, Springer-Verlag (PubID: 822323)

S. Feng, K. Stouffer, K. Jurrens, *"Manufacturing Planning and Predictive Process Models Integration Using Software Agents"* Advanced Engineering Informatics, Vol. 19, pp. 135-142 (PubID: 822324)

S. Fenves, S. Foufou, C. Bock, R. Sriram, *"CPM: A Core Model for Product Data"* Journal of Computing and Information Science in Engineering (PubID: 822334)

M. Gruninger, J. Kopena, *"Semantic Integration through Invariants"* AI Magazine, Vol. 26: 1, pp. 11-20 (PubID: 822315)

C. McLean, S. Jain, Y.T. T. Lee, F. Riddick, *"A Simulation and Gaming Architecture for Manufacturing Research, Testing, and Training"* NIST Interagency/Internal Report (NISTIR 7256) (PubID: 822307)

R. Tongia, E. Subrahmanian, V. Arunachalam, *"Information and Communications Technology for Sustainable Development: Defining a Global Research Agenda"* Allied Publishers, Bangalore (PubID: 822313)

C. Bock, M. Gruninger, *"Messaging in the Process Specification Language"* NIST Interagency/Internal Report (NISTIR 7258) (PubID: 822321)

J. Lubell, B. Kulvatunyou, *"A Tool Kit for Implementing XML Schema Naming and Design Rules"* Proceedings of XML 2005

(PubID: 822319)

Y. Son, B. Kulvatunyou, H. Cho, S. Feng, *"A Semantic Web Service and Simulation Framework to Intelligent Distributed Manufacturing"* Proceedings of the 2005 ASME International Mechanical Engineering Congress and Exposition (PubID: 822322)

M. Baysal, U. Roy, S. Rachuri, R. Sriram, K. Lyons, *"Product Information Exchange Using Open Assembly Model: Issues Related to Representation of Geometric Information"* Proceedings of the 2005 ASME International Mechanical Engineering Congress and Exposition, IMECE 2005, Orlando, FL (PubID: 822621)

X. Zha, S. Foufou, S. Rachuri, R. Sriram, *"Analysis and Evaluation for STEP-Based Electro-Mechanical Assemblies"* Journal of Computing and Information Science (PubID: 822305)

S. Jain, S. K. Leong, *"Stress Testing a Supply Chain Using Simulation"* Proceedings of the 2005 Winter Simulation Conference (PubID: 822304)

X. Zha, R. Sriram, *"Distributed Modeling and Framework for Collaborative Embedded System Design"* Proceedings of the DETC '2005 ASME Design Engineering Technical Conference, Long Beach, CA (PubID: 822301)

X. Zha, R. Sriram, S. Gupta, *"Information and Knowledge Modeling for Computer Supported Micro Electro-Mechanical Systems Design and Development"* Proceedings of the DETC '2005 ASME Design Engineering Technical Conference, Long Beach, CA (PubID: 822297)

Y.T. T. Lee, Y. Luo, *"Data Transfer Strategy for Machine Shop Simulation"* NIST Interagency/Internal Report (NISTIR 7239) (PubID: 822293)

Y.T. T. Lee, Y. Luo, G. Shao, *"Prototype Implementation Based on the Machine Shop Information Model"* Proceedings of the 2005 IFIP5.7 Conference, Rockville, MD (PubID: 822292)

P. Meade, L. Rabelo, A. Jones, *"Applications of Chaos and Complexity Theories to the Technology Adoption Life Cycle"* International Journal of Technology Management (PubID: 822298)

X. Zha, R. Sriram, M. Fernandez, F. Mistree, *"Knowledge-Intensive Collaborative Decision Support for Design Process, Part 1: A Hybrid Decision Model and Multi-Agent Framework"* Journal of Mechanical Design (PubID: 822294)

Y.T. T. Lee, Y. Luo, *"Data Exchange for Machine Shop Simulation"* Proceedings of the 2005 Winter Simulation Conference (PubID: 822296)

N. Ivezic, N. Anicic, A. Jones, Z. Marjanovic, *"Towards Semantic-Based Supply Chain Integration"* Proceedings of the IFIP 5.7 Advances in Production Management Systems Conference, Rockville, MD (PubID: 822295)

C. Bock, *"SysML and UML 2 Support for Activity Modeling"* Journal of the International Council on Systems Engineering, Vol. 9:2, pp. 160-186 (PubID: 822300)

S. Kemmerer, *"Exchanging Technical Product Data, The Story of ISO TC 184/SC4"* NSF NSDL/CODATA Workshop on International Scientific Data, Standards and Digital Libraries, Denver, CO (PubID: 822289)

J. Ramirez-hernandez, H. Li, E. Fernandez, C. McLean, S. K. Leong, *"A Framework for Standard Modular Simulation: Application to Semiconductor Wafer Fabrication"* NIST Interagency/Internal Report (NISTIR 7236) (PubID: 822299)

G. Shao, C. McLean, S. K. Leong, *"A Simulation System with Neutral Data Interface for Shipbuilding Operation"* Proceedings of the Industrial Simulation Conference (PubID: 822284)

Y. Luo, Y.T. T. Lee, *"Application of Machine Shop Data Model in Manufacturing Simulation"* Proceedings of the 2005 International Conference on Modeling, Simulation and Visualization Methods (MSV 05) (PubID: 822283)

C. Xu, S. Gupta, Z. Yao, M. Gruninger, R. Sriram, *"Toward Computer-Aided Conceptual Design of Mechatronic Devices with Multiple Interaction-States"* Proceedings of 2005 ASME Design Engineering Technical Conference, Long Beach, CA (PubID: 822287)

D. Liu, J. Peng, K. Law, G. Wiederhold, R. Sriram, *"Composition of Engineering Web Services with Distributed Data Flows and Computations"* ACM Transactions on Internet Technology Journal (PubID: 822277)

C. Bock, *"UML 2 Activity and Action Models, Part 6: Structured Activities"* Journal of Object Technology, Vol. 4:4, pp. 43-66 (PubID: 822276)

N. Anicic, N. Ivezic, A. Jones, *"An Architecture for Semantic Enterprise Application Integration Standards"* Interoperability of Enterprise Software and Applications, Springer, Edited by D. Konstantas, J.P. Bourrieres, and M. Leonard (PubID: 822281)

S. Rachuri, M. Baysal, U. Roy, S. Foufou, C. Bock, S. Fenves, E. Subrahmanian, K. Lyons, R. Sriram, *"Information Models for Product Representation: Core and Assembly Models"* International Journal of Product Development (PubID: 822266)

S. Foufou, S. Fenves, C. Bock, S. Rachuri, R. Sriram, *"A Core Product Model for PLM with an Illustrative XML Implementation"* Proceedings of the International Conference on PLM, Lyons, France (PubID: 822265)

E. Subrahmanian, S. Rachuri, S. Fenves, S. Foufou, R. Sriram, *"Product Lifecycle Management Support: A Challenge in Supporting Product Design and Manufacturing in a Networked Economy"* NIST Interagency/Internal Report (NISTIR 7211) (PubID: 822275)

B. Kulvatunyou, N. Ivezic, A. Jones, *"Content-Level Conformance Testing: An Information Mapping Case Study"* Proceedings of the Testcom 2005 Conference, Montreal, Canada (PubID: 822271)

L. Patil, D. Dutta, R. Sriram, *"Ontology-based Exchange of Product Data Semantics"* IEEE Transactions on Automation Science and Engineering (PubID: 822263)

E. Subrahmanian, S. Rachuri, S. Fenves, S. Foufou, R. Sriram, *"Challenges in Supporting Product Design and Manufacturing in a Networked Economy: A PLM Perspective"* Proceedings of the International Conference on Product Lifecycle Managment - PLM) (PubID: 822264)

S. Fenves, S. Foufou, C. Bock, N. Bouillon, R. Sriram, *"CPM 2: A Revised Core Product Model for Representing Design Information"* NIST Interagency/Internal Report (NISTIR 7185) (PubID: 822234)

A. Jones, A. Deshmukh, *"Test Beds for Complex Systems"* Special Issue of Communications of the ACM on Complex Adaptive Enterprises (PubID: 822229)

C. McLean, Y.T. T. Lee, G. Shao, F. Riddick, *"Shop Data Model and Interface Specification"* NIST Interagency/Internal Report (NISTIR 7198) (PubID: 822254)

S. Feng, H. Helaakoski, H. Haapasalo, J. Kipina, *"Software Agents-Enabled Systems Coalition for Integrated Manufacturing Processes and Supply Chain Management"* International Journal of Manufacturing Technology and Management - Special Issue on Modeling and Optimization of Supplier-based Manufacturing and Management (PubID: 822258)

C. Dartigues, P. Ghodous, M. Gruninger, D. Pallez, R. Sriram, *"CAD/CAPP Integration using Feature Ontology"* Journal of CAD (PubID: 822256)

S. Rachuri, M. Baysal, U. Roy, S. Foufou, S. Fenves, E. Subrahmanian, K. Lyons, R. Sriram, C. Bock, *"Information Models for Product Representation: Core and Assembly Models"* NIST Interagency/Internal Report (NISTIR 7173) (PubID: 822225)

K. Morris, B. Kulvatunyou, S. P. Frechette, J. Lubell, P. Goyal, *"XML Schema Validation Process for CORE.GOV"* NIST Interagency/Internal Report (NISTIR 7187) (PubID: 822226)

X. Zha, R. Sriram, *"Feature-Based Component Model for Design of Embedded Systems"* Proceedings of the 2004 SPIE"s International Symposium on Optics East, Conference on Intelligent Systems in Design and Manufacturing VI (OE111), Philadelphia, PA (PubID: 822214)

R. Kirsch, *"Standards Electronic Automatic Computer (SEAC)"* NIST Interagency/Internal Report (NISTIR 1005) (PubID: 822213)

C. McLean, F. Riddick, Y.T. T. Lee, *"An Architecture and Interfaces for Distributed Manufacturing Simulation"* Special Issue of the Transactions of the Society for Modelling and Simulation International on Applications of Parallel and Distributed Simulation in Industry (PubID: 822212)

S. Umeda, S. Jain, *"Integrated Supply Chain Simulation System (ISSS) -- Modeling Requirements and Design Issues"* NIST Interagency/Internal Report (NISTIR 7180) (PubID: 822211)

C. Bock, *"UML 2 Composition Model"* Journal of Object Technology, Vol. 3:10, pp. 47-73 (PubID: 822209)

B. Kulvatunyou, K. Morris, *"XML Schema Design Quality Test Requirements"* NIST Interagency/Internal Report (NISTIR 7175) (PubID: 822210)

P. Goyal, *"An XML Schema Naming Assister for Elements and Types"* NIST Interagency/Internal Report (NISTIR 7143) (PubID: 822208)

www.ingramcontent.com/pod-product-compliance
Lightning Source LLC
Chambersburg PA
CBHW081855170526
45167CB00007B/3018